Nundo Lal Dey

Geographical Dictionary of Ancient and Mediaeval India with as Appendix on Modern Names of Ancient Indian Geography

Nundo Lal Dey

Geographical Dictionary of Ancient and Mediaeval India with as Appendix on Modern Names of Ancient Indian Geography

ISBN/EAN: 9783337859725

Printed in Europe, USA, Canada, Australia, Japan

Cover: Foto ©Suzi / pixelio.de

More available books at **www.hansebooks.com**

THE

GEOGRAPHICAL DICTIONARY

OF

ANCIENT AND MEDIÆVAL INDIA

WITH AN

APPENDIX

ON

Modern Names of Ancient Indian Geography

BY

NUNDO LAL DEY

Of the Bengal Judicial Service.

Calcutta:

PRINTED AND PUBLISHED BY W. NEWMAN & CO.

AT THE CAXTON STEAM PRINTING WORKS, 1, MISSION ROW.

1899.

DEDICATED

TO

J. L. HERALD, ESQ., C. S.,

Deputy Commissioner of Hazaribagh,

As a token of my high esteem and deep gratitude.

NUNDO LAL DEY.

I.

THE GEOGRAPHICAL DICTIONARY

OF

ANCIENT AND MEDIÆVAL INDIA

BY

NUNDO LAL DEY

the Bengal Judicial Service.

Calcutta:

PRINTED AND PUBLISHED BY W. NEWMAN & CO.

AT THE CAXTON STEAM PRINTING WORKS, 1, MISSION ROW.

1899.

PREFACE.

In publishing this work, my object is to remove the ficulties which readers of the Puráns and other ancient works Hindu and Buddhist literature generally feel in identifying ancient places they come across. Apart from the natural osity which every one feels to know the modern names of ent places, the knowledge imparts a peculiar interest and zest the perusal of ancient Hindu works. For the compilation of s work, I have been indebted to the works of such authorities General Cunningham, Dr. Führer, Fergusson, Beal, Wilson, nter and others; also to the Archæological Reports, the Asiatic earches and the Journals of the Asiatic Society of Bengal. I ve also derived my information from the accounts of pilgrims ere they have generally agreed, and from local traditions. twithstanding the impetus that has been given of late to hæological inquiry, there are many ancient places which have yet been identified. The change in several names that has n brought about by flux of time owing to the subversion of ts and kingdoms, and the changes in the course of rivers, defies e ingenuity of archæologists to identify them. The present book, however, does not mean to discuss the merits of the identifications, but is only intended to be an alphabetical collection of names of such ancient places in India as have been identified with tolerable certainty.

With regard to the arrangement of the names in this work, I sh only observe that, for facility of finding them out, I have lowed the system observed in English lexicography, xcept with regard to the *a* (अ) or *á* (आ) series of initial letters. I have placed the *á* (आ) series after the *a* (अ) series have be hausted, as is done in the *Abhidháns*. If this little

Geographical Dictionary can prove itself of any use or interest to its readers, my labours will be amply rewarded.

I wish to express my sincere thanks to Major F. P. Maynard, M.B., I.M.S., for kindly looking through the final proofs for me.

CHATRA:
District Hazaribagh:
November, 1899.

NUNDO LAL DEY.

List of Ancient Names

OMITTED IN PART I, BUT ADDED IN PART II:

Ancient Names.	Modern Names (See Pt. II)
A.	
Abhisárá	Hazara.
Achinta	Ajunta.
Ajamera	Ajmir.
Anamala	R. Aumi.
Ánandapura	Barnagar.
Ananta-Padmanábha	Trivendrum.
Anomá	R. Aumi.
Anurádhápura	Anuradhapur.
B.	
Bágar-desa	Bikaner.
Bhadrá	R. Wardha.
Bhimarathá	R. Bhima.
Bhimá-sthána	Takht-i-Bhai.
C.	
Chakshu	R. Oxus.
Chandaná	R. Sabarmati.
Chandrávati	Jhalrapattan.
Chatushpitha-parvata.	Assia range.
Chetyagiri	Besnagar.
D.	
Dhanu-tirtha	Paumben passage.
Dhányavatipura	Dharanikota.
Dharmaprishtha	Dharmáranya.
Dhoondra	Amer.
Dwárasamudra	Hullabid.
G.	
Gambhirá	R. Gambhira.
Girikarniká	R. Sabarmati.
Govardhanapura	Goa.
H.	
Hansa-stupa	Jarásandha-ká-Baithak.
Hatyá-harana	Hattia-haran.
J.	
Jálandhara	Jalandhar.
Jasnaul	Bára-Banki.
Jushkapura	Zukur.
K.	
Kachchha	Cutch.
Kakouttha	R. Bagmati.
Kálanjara	Kalinjar.
Kámakoshthi	Kumbhaconum.
Karnávati	Ahmedabad.
Kásyapi-Gangá	R. Sabarmati.
Khetaka	Kaira (Kheda).
Koláhala-parvata	Brahmajoni hill.
Kritavati	R. Sabarmati.
M.	
Maháráshtra	Márátta country.
Mahásala	R. Pranahita.
Mahati	R. Mahi.
Mallára	Travancore.
Mauli-snána	Multan.
Muchilinda	Buddha-kunda.
Mundá	Chhota Nagpur.
N.	
Nava-Gándhára	Candahar.
Nigambodha-tirtha	Nigambod-ghat.
Nila-parvata	Nilgiri.
Nirvindhya	R. Pain-ganga.
P.	
Padmapura	Pámpur.
Pampápura	Bindhyáchal (town)
Paschimodadhi	Arabian Sea.
Payoshni	R. Purti.
Pranitá	R. Pranahita.
Pravijaya	Jyntea.
Punahpuna	R. Punpun.
Pushpapura	Patna.
R.	
Ramgarh-Gaura	Balarampur.
S.	
Sábhramati	R. Sabarmati.
Seka	Kotah.
Serendwipa	Ceylon.
Srikakola	Chikakol.
Sringagiri	Singhari-mat.
Sudharmanagara	Thatun.
Swetá	R. Swat.
T.	
Tungaveni	R. Tungabhadra
Y.	
Yavana-nagara	J[illegible]ar
Yoni-tirtha	Bhimasthana.

Misarrangement of words in Part I.

On Page	5	*Aparántaka*	should be *after*	... ...	Aparanandá.
,, ,,	21	*Gayasirsha*	,, ,, ,,	... ...	Gayánábhi
,, ,,	35	*Karatoyá*	,, ,, ,,	...	Karakalla.
,, ,,	37	*Karnáta*	,, ,, ,,	... ...	Karna-suvarna.
,, ,,	46	*Kuságárapura*	,, ,, ,,	...	Kusabhavanapura.
,, ,,	58	*Meghaváhana*	,, ,, ,,	... ...	Medhávi-tirtha.
,, ,,	62	*Nilájana*	,, ,, ,,	.. ...	Nikai.
,, ,,	65	*Pancha-Prayága*	,, ,, ,,	... ...	Panchanada.
,, ,,	97	*Uranjirá*	,, ,, ,,	...	Uragá.
,, ,,	101	*Várnaávata*	,, ,, ,,	...	Váránasi-kataka.
,, ,,	105	*Vindhyapáda*	,, ,, ,,	..	Vindhyáchala.
,, ,,	106	*Vitastá*	,, ,, ,,	...	Viswamitra-ásrama.

A

GEOGRAPHICAL DICTIONARY

OF

ANCIENT AND MEDIÆVAL INDIA.

ANCIENT NAMES.	MODERN NAMES OR SITUATION.

A.

ABHISÁRI ... Hazara (country), the Abisares of the Greeks. It was conquered by Arjuna (*Mahábhárat* and Cunningham).

ACHCHHODA-SAROVARA ... Achchhávat in Kásmir, described by Bánabhatta in his Kádamvari. It is six miles from Márttanda. The Siddhásrama was situated on the bank of this lake (*Brihat-Náradiya Purána*).

ADHIRÁJA ... Datihá in the Gawalior territory. It was the kingdom of Dantavakra, who was killed by Krishna. The name of Datihá also indicates the place where Dantavakra was killed. The country was conquered by Sahadeva, one of the five Pándavas. A Vaishnava work, quoted by R. K. Roy in his Mahábhárat, places it near Brindaban in the district of Mathura.

AGASTYA-ÁSRAMA ... 1. Twenty-four miles to the south-east of Násik, now called Agastipuri: it was the hermitage of Rishi Agastya. 2. Kol-

ANCIENT NAMES.	MODERN NAMES OR SITUATION.
	hapur in the province of Bombay. 3 Sarai-Aghat, forty-three miles south-west of Itah in the North-Western Provinces (Führer's *Monumental Antiquities and Inscriptions*).
AGRAVANA ...	Agra, one of the eighty-four *vanas* of Vraja.
AHICHCHHATRA.	Ramnagar, twenty miles west of Bareli. The name of Ahichchhatra is at present confined to the great fortress in the lands of Alampur Kot and Nasratganj. It was the capital of north Panchála or Rohilkhand (Dr. Führer and General Cunningham).
AHICHHATRA ...	Same as *Ahichchhatra.*
AHIKSHETRA ...	Same as *Ahichchhatra.*
AIRÁVATI ...	The river Ravi. The Rapti and Irawadi are also the contractions of this name.
AJAMATI ...	The river Ajaya in Bengal.
AJITAVATI ...	The Little Gandak river on the north of Kusinagara (Kasia), where Buddha died. The river is also called Hiranyavati.
AKHANDHA ...	Dildarnagar, twelve miles south of Ghazipur.
AMARAKANTAKA	It is a part of the Mikul (Mekala) hills, in which the rivers Nerbuda and Sone have got their source.

ANCIENT NAMES.	MODERN NAMES OR SITUATION.
AMARANÁTHA ...	A celebrated temple of Siva in a grotto "full of wonderful congelations" in the Haramuk mountain of the Bhairavagháti range of the Himalaya in Kásmir (Bernier's *Travels*, *note*, p. 418). It is open to the pilgrims in the month of Srában who visit the shrine escorted by officers in the service of the Mahárájá of Kásmir. A miraculous pigeon-like bird is said to appear every year, gyrating and fluttering over the temple, to the amazed gaze of the assembled pilgrims.
AMARÁVATI ...	1. Nagarhára, about two miles to the west of Jallálábad: a village close to it is still called Nagarak (Na-kie of Fa Hian) V. St. Martin. 2. Amraoti in Central India.
AMARESWARA ...	Omkárnáth, where the temple of Omkárnáth, one of the twelve great Lingas of Mahádeva, is situated. It is near Mandaleswar, five miles to the east of Mahes (ancient Máhishmati), on the right bank of the Nerbuda, and two miles to the east of the Kheri station of the R. M. Railway. The twelve great Lingas are: Somanáth in Sauráshtra, Mallikárjuna in Srisaila, Mahá-kála in Ujjaini, Omkára in Amareswara, Kedára in the Himalaya, Bhimasankara in Dákini, Biseswara in Benares, Tryambaka in Gomati, Baidyanátha in Chitábhumi, Náges in Dwáraká, Rámeswara in Setubandha, and Ghusrines in Siválaya.

ANCIENT NAMES.	MODERN NAMES OR SITUATION.
AMBARA ...	The country of Jeypur, so called from its ancient capital of that name, now called Ámer.
AMI ...	Eleven miles east of Chhapra, containing a temple of Bhaváni, which is one of the 52 Pithas, where a fragment from the body of Sati is said to have fallen.
ANAHILAPATTANA ...	Pattana in Guzerat, founded in the eighth century of the Christian era by Banaraj.
ANDHRA ...	1. The country between the Godávari and the Krishna. Its capital was Dhanakataka. Vengi, five miles to the north of Ellur, was, according to Beal, its ancient capital. 2. Telingana, south of Hyderabad.
ANGA ...	The country about Bhagalpur. Its capital was Champápuri. Its western boundary was the junction of the Ganges and the Saraju. It was the kingdom of Lomapáda of the Rámáyana and Karna of the Mahábhárat.
ANTRAVEDA ...	The Doab between the Ganges and the Jamuná.
ANUPA-DESA ...	1. Mhow in Malwa. 2. Same as *Haihaya*.
AORNOS (OF THE GREEKS) ...	Ránighat, sixteen miles north of Ohind, according to Cunningham, but according to Captain James Abbot, Shah Kote on Mount Mahában, situated on the western bank of the Indus.

ANCIENT NAMES.		MODERN NAMES OR SITUATION.
APAGA	...	The Ayuk-nadi to the west of the Rávi in the Panjab.
APARANANDA	...	A small stream called the Sukrinadi which flows through the districts of Gaya and Patna, and falls into the Ganges.
APARA-VIDEHA	...	Rungpur and Dinajpur (Dr. R. L. Mitra).
APARÁNTAKA	...	Konkan and Malabar.
ARBUDA	...	Mount Abu in the Aravali range in Rajputana. It was the hermitage of Rishi Vasishtha. It contains the celebrated Jain temple dedicated to Rishava Deva.
ARDHAGANGA	...	The river Kaveri.
ARJIKIYA	...	The river Beas (Vipasá).
ARJUNI	...	The river Báhudá (Dhabalá).
ARKAKSHETRA	...	Same as *Padmakshetra*.
ARUNAKUNDA-PURA	...	Warrangal, the ancient capital of Telingana.
ASHTABAKRA-ÁSRAMA	...	Ráhugráma (now called Raila), ten miles from Hardwar, near which flows the Ashtabakra-nadi, a small river, perhaps the ancient Samangá.
ASIKNI	...	The river Chenab (Chandrabhágá).
ASWA-TIRTHA	...	The confluence of the Ganges and the Kálinadi in the district of Kánouj (*Prakriti-vádá*).

ANCIENT NAMES.		MODERN NAMES OR SITUATION.
AUDUMVARA	...	Cutch, its ancient capital was Koteswara or Kachchheswara.
AVANTI	...	1. Ougein. 2. The country of which Ougein was the capital. It was the kingdom of Vikramáditya: Malwa.
AVANTI-NADI	...	The Siprá. Ougein stands on this river.
AYODHANA	...	Pák-Pattana in the Panjab.
AYODHYÁ	...	Oudh, the kingdom of Ráma. During the Buddhist period, Ayodhyá was divided into Uttara (Northern) Kosala and Dakshina (Southern) Kosala. The river Saraju divided the two provinces. The capital of the former was Srávasti on the Rápti, and the capital of the latter was Ayodhyá on the Saraju. The ancient capital of the kingdom was also called Ayodhyá, the birth-place of Ráma. At a place in the town called Janmasthána he was born; at a place called Tretá-ki-Thákur he performed the horse-sacrifice, by setting up the image of Sitá; at Swargadwáram his body was burned. Ádináth, a Jaina Tirthankar, was born at Ayodhyá (Führer).
ADIKOTA	...	Another name of *Ahichchhatra*.
ÁLAVI	...	Airwá, an ancient Buddhist town, the A-lo of Fa Hian, twenty-seven miles north-east of Itawah. It is the Álabhi of the Jainas, from which Mahávira made his missionary peregrinations (Führer).
ANARTTA	...	Guzerát and part of Malwa.

ANCIENT NAMES.	MODERN NAMES OR SITUATION.
ÁRAMANAGARA ..	Arrah in the district of Shahabad.
ÁRATTA ...	The Panjab.
ÁRYÁVARTTA ...	The northern part of India which lies between the Himalaya and the Vindhyá range.
ÁSILDURGA ...	Junágar (Tod).
ÁYUDHA ...	The country that lies between the Vitastá (Jhelum) and the Sindhu (Indus).

B

BADARIKÁ-ÁSRAMA ...	Badrináth. The temple of Nara-Náráyana is built on the bank of the Bishen-gangá (Alakánandá) over the site of a hot-spring called Tapanakunda, the existence of which, no doubt, led to the original selection of this remote spot (*Asiatic Researches*, Vol. XVI). It was the hermitage of the celebrated Rishi Vyása.
BAIDURYA-PARVATA ..	The Satpura hills.
BAIDYUTA ...	A part of the Kailas range, at the foot of which the Manas-sarovara lake is situated.
BAKRESWARI ...	The river Báblá which falls into the Ganges near Katwa in the district of Burdwan.
BALABHI ...	In Guzerát near Bhaonagar.

ANCIENT NAMES.	MODERN NAMES OR SITUATON.
BALLÁLABARI ..	The capital of Ballála Sena, king of Bengal, now called Rámpála, about two miles from Munshigunge at Vikrampur in the district of Dacca. The remains of Ballála Sena's fort still exist at this place.
BANAPURA ...	Mahábalipur or the Seven Pagodas on the Coromandel Coast.
BANGA ...	Bengal. Bengal was divided into five provinces: Pundra or North Bengal; Samatata or East Bengal; Kámarupa or Assam; Támralipta or South Bengal; and Karna-Suvarna or West Bengal (R. C. Dutt).
BANSAGULMA ..	A sacred reservoir (*kund*) on the table-land of Amarakantaka, which is situated on the east, about four miles and a half, of the source or first fall of the Nerbuda.
BARADÁNA-TIRTHA ...	Baroda, where Rishi Durvásá gave a boon to Vishnu.
BASUDHARA-TIRTHA ...	The place where the Alakánandá has got its source, about four miles north of Badrináth, near the village Manal.
BAHUDA ...	The river Dhabalá, now called Dhumela or Burha-Rápti, a feeder of the Rápti in Oudh. The severed arm of Rishi Likhita grew when he bathed in this river: hence the river is called Báhudá.

ANCIENT NAMES.		MODERN NAMES OR SITUATION.
BHARADWÁJA-ÁSRAMA	...	Allahabad: the hermitage of Rishi Bharadwája. The image of the Rishi is worshipped in a temple built on the site of his hermitage at Colonelganj. The hermitage was visited by Rámachandra on his way to the Dandakáranya.
BHARU-KACHCHHA	...	Baroach, the Barygaza of the Greeks. Bali Rájá, attended by his priest Sukráchárya, performed a sacrifice at this place, when he was deprived of his kingdom by Vishnu in the shape of a dwarf (Vámana).
BHAGANAGARA		Hyderabad.
BHÁGAPRASTHA		Bágpat, thirty miles to the west of Mirat, one of the five *prasthas* or villages demanded by Yudhishthira from Duryodhana.
BHÁGAVATI	...	The river Bágmati in Nepal: Kakouttha of the Buddhists (Lassen).
BHÁRATAVARSHA	...	India. India (Intu of Hiuen Tsiang) is a corruption of Sindhu or Sapta Sindhu (Hafta Hindu of the Arabs).
BHIMANAGARA	..	Kangra.
BHIMAPURA	...	Vidarbhanagara or Kundinapura, the capital of Vidarbha.
BHIMARATHI	...	The river Bhimá which joins the Krishna.

ANCIENT NAMES.	MODERN NAMES OR SITUATION.
BHOJAKATA-PURA ...	The second capital of Vidarbha, founded by Rukmi, the brother of Rukmini who was the wife of Krishna. A writer in the Asiatic Researches says it was situated near Mozaffarnagar. It is perhaps Ellichpur on the river Purná in Berar.
BHOJAPURA ...	Same as *Bhojakatapura*.
BHOTANGA ...	Bhootan.
BHRIGU-ÁSRAMA	1. Balia, in the N.-W. Provinces, said to have been the capital of Rájá Bali. Báwán, six miles west of Hardoi in Oudh, also claims the honor of being the capital of Bali Rájá, who was deprived of his kingdom by Vishnu in his Vámana-avatár. Bhrigu Rishi once performed his asceticism at Balia: there is a temple dedicated to the Rishi, which is frequented by pilgrims. Balia was once situated at the confluence of the Ganges and the Saraju; it was called Bágrásan, being a contraction of Bhrigu-ásrama. 2. Baroach was also the hermitage of this Rishi.
BHRIGU-KACHCHHA ...	Same as *Bharukachchha*, which is a corruption of Bhrigukshetra, as it was the residence of Bhrigu Rishi (*Bhagvat Purán*).
BIBHÁNDAKA-ASRAMA ...	Same as *Rishyasringa-ásrama*.

ANCIENT NAMES.	MODERN NAMES OR SITUATION.
BINASANA-TIRTHA ..	The spot in the great sandy desert in the district of Sirhind where the river Saraswati loses itself after taking a westerly course from Thaneswar.
BINA ...	The river Krishna, the Tynna of the Greeks. It is also called Venwá.
BINDU-SARA ..	1. A sacred pool situated at the Rudra-Himalaya, two miles south of Gangotri, where Bhagiratha is said to have performed asceticism for bringing down the goddess Gangá from heaven. 2. Sitpur in Guzerát, north-west of Ahmedabad: it was the hermitage of Karddama Rishi and birth-place of Kapila.
BINGAR ...	Ahmednagar, seventy-one miles from Poona, which was founded by Ahmed Nizam Shah in 1494.
BIRAJÁ-KSHETRA	The country which stretches for ten miles around Jajpur on the bank of the river Baitarani in Orissa.
BITHABHAYA-PATTANA ...	Bitha, eleven miles south-west of Allahabad.
BOLOR ...	Baltistan or Little Thibet.
BRAHMAKUNDA	The *kunda* from which the river Brahmaputra issues: it is a place of pilgrimage.
BRAHMANÁLA ...	Manikarnika in Benares.

ANCIENT NAMES.	MODERN NAMES OR SITUATION.
BRAHMARSHI ...	The country between Brahmávartta and the river Jamuná: it comprised Kurukshetra, Matsya, Panchála and Surasena.
BRAHMA-TIRTHA	Pushkara lake.
BRAHMÁVARTTA	The country between the rivers Saraswati and Drisadvati (Manu).
BUDDHAVANA ...	Budhain, about six miles north of Tapoban in the district of Gaya.
BUKEPHALA (OF THE GREEKS) ...	Jalálpur in the Panjab (Cunningham).

C.

CHAKRA-TIRTHA	1. In Kurukshetra, much resorted to at the time of Mahmud of Ghazni. 2. In Prabhása in Guzerát. 3. Six miles from the village called Tryamvaka, which is near the source of the Godávari.
CHAMPÁPURI ...	Champánagar near Bhagalpur: it was the ancient capital of Anga.
CHANDANA-GIRI	The Malaya-giri,—the Malabar Ghâts.
CHANDAPURA ..	Chayenpur, five miles to the west of Bhabua in the district of Shahabad. The celebrated battle described in the Chandi between Kali and the two kings, Sumbha and Nisumbha, is said to have been fought at this place. The Márkandeya Purána, however, places the scene of the battle in the Himalaya. The name of Chandapur is derived from the name of one of the two brothers, Chanda and Munda, who were the generals of the kings.

ANCIENT NAMES.	MODERN NAMES OR SITUATION.
CHANDELGARA ..	Chunar. The name of Chandelgara has been derived from the Chandels, a tribe of Kshatriyas who had established their sway between Mirzapur and the district of Shahabad (see *Charanádri*).
CHANDRABHÁGÁ	The Chenab,—the Ascesines of the Greeks.
CHANDRAGIRI ...	Near Belligola, not far from Seringapatam, sacred to the Jainas.
CHANDRÁVATI ...	The river Gogá which falls into the Ganges.
CHANDRIKÁ ...	The river Chandrabhágá (Chenab)
CHANDRIKAPURI	Srávasti or Sahet-mahet: it was the birth-place of Chandraprabhánátha, the eighth Tirthankara of the Jains.
CHANDWAR ...	Firozabad, near Agra, where in 1193 Shahabuddin Ghori defeated Jaya Chandra, king of Kanouj. Chandwar is evidently a contraction of Chandrapura.
CHARANADRI ..	Chunar in the district of Mirzapur. The hill-fort of Chunar was at one time considered one of the most impregnable forts in India. It was built by the Pál Rájás, who reigned over Bengal and Behar from the middle of the ninth to the twelfth century of the Christian era. The portion of the fort, which is called Bhatrihari's palace, is the place where he performed asceticism. The fort is said to have been protected by the goddess Gangá Devi all the day, except in the first *prahar* of the morning.

ANCIENT NAMES.	MODERN NAMES OR SITUATION.
CHARITRAPURA	Puri in Orissa (Cunningham).
CHARMANAVATI	The river Chambal.
CHATTALA	Chittagong. The temple of Bhavâni on the Chandrasekhara hill near Sitakunda is one of the 52 Pithas, where a portion of Sati's right hand is said to have fallen.
CHEDI ...	According to Tod, Chanderi, a town in Malwa, was the capital of Sisupála, who was killed by Krishna (see also *J. A. S. B.*, Vol. XV). According to Dr. Führer, Dahala Mandala was the ancient Chedi. According to some, it comprised the southern portion of Bundelkhand and northern portion of Jabbalpur: Rewa. Kálanjara was the capital of Chedi under the Gupta kings. Chedi was also called Tripuri.
CHERA ...	It comprised Travancore, part of Malabar, and Coimbatoor.
CHITABHUMI ...	Baidyanáth,—one of the 52 Pithas. It contains the temples of the goddess Jayadurgá and her Bhairava Baidyanáth.
CHITRADURGA ..	Chitteldoorg.
CHITRA-KUTA ...	Kámptánáth-giri in Bundelkhand: it is an isolated hill on a river called the Paisuni (Payoswini) or Mandákini, where Ráma dwelt for some time during his exile. It is twelve miles from Markund and fifty miles south-east of Banda.

ANCIENT NAMES.	MODERN NAMES OR SITUATION.
CHITRAPALÁ ...	The river Mahanadi in Orissa.
CHITROTPALÁ ...	Same as *Chitrapalá.*
CHOLA ...	The Coromandel Coast, between the rivers Kaveri and Krishna. Its capital was Kánchi or Kánchipura. Chola was also called Drávida.
CHYABANA-ASRAMA ...	Chausa in the district of Shahabad: the hermitage of Rishi Chyabana. 2. The hermitage of the Rishi was also situated on the Satpura mountains. 3. Dhosi, six miles south of Nárnol in the Jeypur territory, where the Rishi's eyes are said to have been pierced by a princess of Anupadesa, whom he afterwards married.

D

DAKSHINA-GANGA ...	The river Godávari.
DAKSHINA-MATHURÁ ...	Madura in the province of Madras. It was also called Mathurá and Minákshi. It was the capital of the ancient kingdom of Pándya or Pándu. It is one of the 52 Pithas where Sati's eyes are said to have fallen.
DAKSHINA-PATHA ...	The Deccan at the time of Bhavabhuti was called by the name of Dakshinapatha. It is the Dandakáranya of the Rámáyana.

ANCIENT NAMES.		MODERN NAMES OR SITUATION.
DAKSHINA-PRAYAGA	...	Triveni on the north of Hugli in Bengal (Raghunandana).
[illegible]	...	Rájmahendri on the Godavari, according [illegible] ngham and McCrindle; but some [illegible] pur in Orissa. Hunter [illegible] place where [illegible] rds [illegible] of Bu[illegible] and enshrined [illegible] Kalinga, shortly after his de[illegible]
DARADA	...	Dardistan, north of Kásmir, on th[illegible] upper bank of the Indus.
DARBHAVATI		Dabhoi in Guzerát (Burgess), and according to Führer, Dibhai, twenty-six miles south-west of Bulandsahar. Dibhai was the Rhodopha of the Greeks.
DARDARA		The southern portion of the Eastern Gháts (*Raghuvansa*).
DASAPURA	...	Mandasor in Malwa.
DASARNA	...	A part of the Chhatisgarh district. The *Desarina Regio* of the Periplus was between Masalia or Maslipatam and the mouth of the Ganges (Wilson).
DÁKSHINÁTYA	...	The Deccan: that part of India which lies to the south of the Vindhyá range
DÁMALIPTA	...	Is a corruption of Támralipta: it was the capital of Sumha (see *Sumha*).
DAMODARA	...	The river Damuda in Bengal.

ANCIENT NAMES.	MODERN NAMES OR SITUATION.
DEVABANDARA...	Diu in Guzerát.
DEVAGARA ...	Same as *Dharagara*.
DEVAGIRI .	Part of the Aravali range.
DEVIKOTA ...	Same as *Sonitapura*.
DEVI-PATAN ...	Forty-six miles north-east of Gonda in Oudh: it is one of the 52 Pithas where Sati's right arm is said to have fallen.
DEWALA	Tatta in Scind (Tod).
DHANAKATAKA...	Dharanikota, which is one mile to the west of Amarávati: it was at one time the name of the district (Beal). Fergusson identifies it with Bejwada. Dhanakataka or Dharanikota was the capital of Raja Satavahana or Sáliváhana and his descendants.
DHANAPURA ...	Johargan}, twenty-four miles from Ghazipur (Führer).
DHARAGARA ...	Dowlatabad in Hyderabad: the Tagara of the Greeks.
DHARMAPATTANA	Srávasti, or the present village of Sahetmahet: it was the capital of north Kosala.
DHARMAPURA ...	Dharampur, north of Nasik.
DHARMÁRANYA...	1. Four miles from Buddha-Gayá in the district of Gaya. It is the Dharmáranya of the Buddhist records, visited by numerous pilgrims (*List of Ancient*

ANCIENT NAMES.	MODERN NAMES OR SITUATION.
	Monuments in the Patna Division, p 64'. A temple sacred to Dharmmeswara exists at this place. 2. By some it is considered to have comprised portions of the districts of Balia and Ghazipur (Dr. Führer's *Monumental Antiquities and Inscriptions*, p. 191).
DHARMODAYA ...	The river Dámudá in Bengal (McCrindle).
DHÁRÁNAGARA...	Dhár in Malwa, the capital of Rájá Bhoja
DRÁVIDA ...	Part of the Deccan from Madras to Seringapatam and Cape Comorin. Its capital was Kánchipura (see *Chola*).
DRISADVATI ...	The Caggar (Ghágar) which flowed through Ambala and Sirhind, now lost in the sands of Rajputana (Elphinstone and Tod).
DUD-GANGÁ ...	The river Dauli, a branch of the Alakánandá.
DURJAYALINGA...	Darjiling, which contains a temple of the Mahadeo called Durjayalinga. Darjiling is a corruption of Durjayalinga.
DURVÁSÁ-ÁSRAMA	1. The hermitage of Rishi Durvásá is pointed out in the Colgong hills at the distance of about a mile from the town of Colgong in the district of Bhagalpur. 2. Durvásá's hermitage was also at Dubáur, in the hills, seven miles south-east of Rajauli, in the sub-division of Nowadah, in the district of Gaya (Grierson's *Notes on the District of Gaya*).

ANCIENT NAMES.		MODERN NAMES OR SITUATION.
DWÁRAKESI	...	Same as *Dwárikeswari*.
DWÁRÁVATI	...	1. Dwarka in Guzerát. Krishna made it his capital after his flight from Mathura. 2. Siam (Phayre).
DWÁRIKÁ	...	Dwarka in Guzerát.
DWÁRIKESWARI		The river Dalkisor near Bishnupur in Bengal, one of the branches of the Rupnáráyana.

E

EKACHAKRÁ	...	Arrah, according to Cunningham (*Arch. Report*, 1871-72, Vol. III). But this identification is very doubtful. Dr. Führer has identified it with Chakarnagar, sixteen miles south-west of Itawah.
EKÁMRAKÁNANA		Bhuvaneswara in Orissa (see *Harakshetra*).

G

GAHALATA	...	Ghilghit (McCrindle).
GANDAKI	...	The river Gandak. It rises in the Sapta Gandaki or Dhawalagiri range of the Himalaya, which is the southern boundary of Central Thibet, and enters the plains at a spot called Tribeni *Ghát*. The source of the river is not far from Sálagráma, which was the hermitage of Bharata and Pulaha. The temple of Muktinátha (an image of Náráyana) s

ANCIENT NAMES.	MODERN NAMES OR SITUATION.
	on the south of Sálagráma. Hence the river is called also Sálagrámi and Náráyani (*Brahmavaivartta Purána*).
GANDHA-HASTI STUPA ...	Bakraur on the Phalgu, opposite to Buddha-Gayá, visited by Hiuen Tsiang.
GANDHAMÁDANA	A part of the Rudra Himalaya. The range of Gandhamádana commences at a short distance to the north-east of Badarikásrama.
GANDHARAVA-DESA	Gándhára, which is evidently a corruption of Gandharáva-desa (see *Gándhára*).
GANGÁ ...	The Ganges.
GANGÁDWÁRA ..	Haridwar (see *Máyápuri*).
GANGOTRI ...	A spot in the Rudra-Himalaya, in Gurwal, supposed by the ancient Hindus to have been the source of the Ganges, though it has been traced further north by Captain Hodgson (*Asiatic Researches*, Vol. XIV). There is a temple of Gangá Devi. One kos from Gangotri and two kos from Meani-ki-Gadh, there is a spot called Patangni, which is noted as the place where the five Pándavas remained for twelve years worshipping Mahádeo. After that period they left this place and ascended Swargarohini, a peak of the sacred hill, whence the Ganges flows: there four of the brothers died. The Rudra-Himalaya has five principal peaks

ANCIENT NAMES.	MODERN NAMES OR SITUATION.
	called Rudra-Himalaya (the eastern peak), Burrampoori, Bissenpoori, Ood-gurrikanta, and Swargarohini (the western and nearest peak). These form a sort of semi-circular hollow of very considerable extent filled with eternal snow, from the gradual dissolution of the lower parts of which the principal part of the stream is generated (Fraser's *Himala Mountains*). See *Sumeru-parvata*.
GARGA-ÁSRAMA	The reputed site of the hermitage of Rishi Garga is situated in the Rai Bareli district, opposite to Ásni, across the Ganges.
GARJAPURA	Ghazipur. This part of the country was visited by Fa Hian in the fifth century. Cunningham infers the ancient name of Garjapura from the modern name of Ghazipur.
GAURA ...	See *Goura*.
GAUTAMA-ÁSRAMA ...	1. Ahalyásthána in the village of Ahiari, pargana Jarail, twenty-four miles to the south-west of Janakpur in Tirhut. 2. Godná or Revelganj near Chhapra. 3. Áhiroli near Buxar. The Rámáyana, however, places the hermitage of the Rishi Gautama near Janakpur.
GAUTAMI	The river Godávari.
GAYASIRSHA	1. Gayá. 2. The mount Gayasirsha, called Gayasisa in the Buddhist annals, is the Brahmayoni hill in Gayá, where

ANCIENT NAMES.	MODERN NAMES OR SITUATION.
	Buddha preached his "burning" sermon called the Sermon of the Mount (Monier Williams' *Buddhism*).
GAYÁ ...	It is situated between the Rámsilá hill on the north and the Brahmayoni hill on the south, on the bank of the river Phalgu. The town is composed of the modern town of Shahebganj on the northern side, and the ancient town of Gayá on the southern side. In the southern portion of the town is situated the celebrated temple of Vishnupada, which was erected some two hundred years ago by Ahalyá-bái, the daughter-in-law of Mulhar Rao Holkar of Indore, on the site of a more ancient temple. The temple of Mangalá-Gouri, one of the 52 Pithas, where Sati's breast is said to have fallen, is situated on a spur of the Brahmayoni range called the Bháshnáth. Buddha-Gayá (see *Uravilwa* is six miles to the south of Gayá.
GAYÁNÁBHI ...	Jájpur in Orissa. Gayásura, a demon who was overthrown by Vishnu, was of such a bulky stature that when stretched on the ground his head rested at Gayá, his navel at Jájpur, and his feet at a place near Rajmahendri.
GÁDHIPURA ...	Kánouj. It was the capital of Gádhi Rájá, the father of Rishi Viswámitra.
GÁLAVA-ÁSRAMA	The hermitage of Rishi Gálava, three miles from Jeypur

ANCIENT NAMES.	MODERN NAMES OR SITUATION.
GÁNDHÁRA ...	The country of Gándhára lies along the Kábul river between the Khoaspes (Kunar) and the Indus. Its capital was Purushapura, now called Peshawur (Beal). Ptolemy makes the Indus the eastern boundary of the *Gandari*. It is the Kiantolo of Hiuen Tsiang, the *Kundara Gandaridæ* of Strabo and other ancient Greek geographers. In the Ayín Akbari it forms the district of Pukely, lying between Kásmir and Attock (*J. A. S. B.*, Vol. XV). Gándhára comprised the modern districts of Peshawur and Hoti Murdan, or what is called the Eusofzai country, where discoveries were made of excellent Buddhist architecture and sculptures of the time of Kaniksha, *i.e.*, of the first century of the Christian era, at Ranigat, Sanghao and Nuttu, through the labours of Major Cole (*Memorandum of Ancient Monuments in Eusofzai*). Pushkarávati or Pushkalávati (Pukely) was its ancient capital, which the Rámáyana placed in Gandharva-desa. Gándhára of the Mahábhárat and the Buddhist period, therefore, is the corruption of Gandharva-desa of Válmiki.
GEHAMURA	Gahmar (E. I. Railway) in the district of Ghazipur. It was the abode of Mura, a *daitya*, who was killed by Krishna (Führer).
GIRINAGARA ..	Girnár, one of the hills known by the name of Junágar hills, at a very little distance from the town of Junágar,

ANCIENT NAMES.	MODERN NAMES OR SITUATION.
	sacred to the Jains as containing the temples of Neminàth and Páraswanáth. It was the hermitage of Rishi Dattátreya.
GIRIVRAJAPURA	Rájgir in Behar, the ancient capital of Magadha, where Jarásandha's palace was situated. It is surrounded by five hills called in the Mahábhárat Vaiháṛa, Varáha, Vrishabha, Rishi-giri, and Chaityaka, but they are now called Baibhár-giri, Vipula-giri, Ratna-giri, Udaya-giri, and Sona-giri. Vaihára has been identified with Baibhár-giri, Rishi-giri with Ratna-giri, and Chaityaka with Vipula-giri. *Rangbhum* in Jarásandha's fort is pointed out as the spot where Bhima killed Jarásandha. The first Buddhist Synod was held in 477 B. C. on the southern slope of the Baibhár hill in front of the Son-bhándár cave formerly called the Sattapanni cave, where Buddha used to live. Just behind the *Baithak* of Jarásandha there is another cave called the Pippali cave, where Buddha used to meditate after his meals. Buddha resided in a cave of the Pándava-giri, which is a spur of the Ratna-giri on the eastern side of the town, when for the first time he came to Rájagriha.
GIRIYEK ...	An ancient Buddhist village on the Panchána river, on the southern border of the district of Patna.
GODÁVARI ...	The river Godávari has got its source in the Brahma-giri mountain, situated on the side of a village called Tryam-

ANCIENT NAMES.		MODERN NAMES OR SITUATION.
		vaka, which is twenty miles from Nasik. Some suppose that the river has got its source in the neighbouring mountain called Jatáphatká. In Tryamvaka there is a tank called Kusávartta, underneath which the Godávari is said to flow after issuing from the mountain. Every twelfth year, pilgrims from all parts of India resort to this village for the purpose of bathing in this sacred tank and worshipping the Mahádeo called Tryamvakeswara.
GOKARNA	....	Gendia, a town in the province of North Canara, thirty miles from Goa (Wilford). It is a celebrated place of pilgrimage. It contains the temple of Mahabaleswara. It is thirty miles south of Sedasheogar, which is three miles south of Goa. (Newbold, *J. A. S. B.*, Vol. XIV, p. 497).
GOMANTA-GIRI	....	An isolated mountain on the northern side of the Western Ghâts, where Krishna and Balaráma defeated Jarásandha (*Harivansa*).
GOMATI		1. The river Gumti in Oudh. 2 The river Godávari.
GOMUKHI	...	Fifteen miles north of Gangotri: a celebrated place of pilgrimage.
GONARDDA	..	The Panjab, from Gonardda, king of Kásmir, who conquered it.
GOPAKAVANA	...	Goa.
GOPRATÁRA	...	Guptára, a place of pilgrimage on the bank of the Saraju at Fyzabad, where Ráma is said to have died

ANCIENT NAMES.	MODERN NAMES OR SITUATION.
GOURA ...	1. The whole of Bengal was so denominated from its capital of the same name, the ruins of which lie near Malda at a distance of about ten miles (see *Lakshmanávati*). 2. Uttara Kosala, the capital of which was Srávasti, was also called Goura. Gondá, a sub-division of Uttara Kosala, forty-two miles south of Srávasti, is evidently a corruption of Goura. The traditions respecting the famous tooth-brush tree (*danta-dhávana*) of Buddha still exist at Gondá (Führer).
GOURI ...	A tributary of the Kabul river.
GOURIKUNDA ...	A holy place at a very short distance from Gangotri, where the Kedar-Gangá debouches into the Bhágirathi (Fraser's *Himala Mountains*).
GOVA-RÁSHTRA ...	Goa.
GRIDHRAKUTA	It is a part of Saila-giri,—the Vulture peak of Fa Hian and Hiuen Tsiang. It lies two miles and-a-half to the south-east of new Rájgir and north-east of old Rájgir. Buddha performed here austerities for some time after leaving the Pándava-giri cave, and in his subsequent sojourn, he delivered here many of his excellent *sutras*.
GUNAMATI-VIHÁRA	The Gunamati monastery, which was visited by Hiuen Tsiang, was situated on the Kunwa hill at Dharáwat in the sub-division of Jahanabad in the district of Gaya. The twelve-armed statue of Bhairab at that place is really an ancient Buddhist statue of Avalokiteswara (Grierson).

ANCIENT NAMES.	MODERN NAMES OR SITUATION.
GURJARA ...	Guzerát. In the seventh century, at the time of Hiuen Tsiang, the name was not extended to the peninsula of Guzerát, which was then known only by the name of Saurásbtra. The modern district of Marwar was then known by the name of Gurjara.

H

HAIHAYA	Khandesh, parts of Aurangabad and South Malwa. It was the kingdom of Kárttaviryárjuna, who was killed by Parasuráma. Its capital was Máhishmati, now called Maheswara or Chuli-Maheswara.
HAIMAVATI ...	Same as *Rishikulyá*.
HARAKSHETRA...	Bhuvaneswara in Orissa. It was the site of a capital city founded by Rájá Yayáti Kesari, who reigned in Orissa in the latter part of the fifth century. The Kesari dynasty consisted of forty-three princes, who ruled over Orissa from 474 to 1132 A. D., after the Yavanas (Hunter's *Orissa*).
HASTINÁPURA ...	The capital of the Kurus, north-east of Delhi, entirely diluviated by the river Ganges. It was situated twenty-two miles north-east of Mirat and south-west of Bijnor, on the right bank of the Ganges. Nichakshu, the grandson of Janmejaya of the Mahábhárat, removed his capital to Kausámbi after the destruction of Hastinápura (*Vishnu-Purána*)

ANCIENT NAMES.	MODERN NAMES OR SITUATION.
HÁRITA-ÁSRAMA	Ekalinga, six miles north of Udaipur in Rajputana (Tod).
HÁTAKA ...	Undes or Hundes, where the lake Mánas-sarovara is situated.
HEMAKUTA ..	The Ratna-giri hill, one of the five hills of Rájgir, in the district of Patna.
HIMAVANTA ...	Thibet.
HIMÁDRI ...	The Himalaya mountains.
HINGULÁ ...	Hinglaj, situated at the extremity of the range of mountains in Baluchistan called by the name of Hingulá, about a day's journey from the sea-coast. The Aghor or Hingulá river passes by its side. It is one of the 52 Pithas or places celebrated as the spots on which the dissevered limbs of Sati were scattered. The temple of Durgá is known here by the name of Mahámáyá or Kottari.
HIRAMBA ...	Cachar.
HIRANYABÁHU...	The river Sone, the Erannoboas of the Greeks.
HIRANYA-PARVATA ...	Monghir (see *Mudgala-giri*).
HIRANYAVATI ...	The little Gandak; same as *Ajitavati*.
HLÁDINI	The river Brahmaputra.
HUPIAN	The capital of Parsusthána, the country of the Parsus, a warlike tribe mentioned by Pánini. Hupian is the present Opian, a little to the north of Charikar at the entrance of a pass over the north-east end of the Pamghan range (Beal).

ANCIENT NAMES.	MODERN NAMES OR SITUATION.
HUSHKAPURA	Shecroh in Lár (Beal); Barámula in Kásmir on the Jhelum (Cunningham).

I

IKSHUMATI ...	The river Káli-nadi in Rohilkhand.
ILBALA	Ellora near Daulatabad, in Central India. Rishi Agastya is said to have killed the *Daityas* Ilbal and his brother Vátápi at this place while on his way to the south (N. C. Das's *Ancient Geography of Asia*).
INDRAPRASTHA	Old Delhi. The city of Indraprastha was built upon the banks of the Jamuná, between the more modern Kotila of Firoz Shah and Humayun's tomb, about two miles south of modern Delhi. The river has now shifted its course more than a mile eastwards. The Nigambod Ghât is believed to have formed a part of the ancient capital. Its name, however, is preserved in that of Indrapat, one of the popular names for the fort of the *Purána Kilá*, which is still pointed out as the fort of Yudishthira and his brothers (*Panjab Gazetteer*). The fort was repaired by Humayun, which he called Dinpánná Indraprastha was the capital of Yudishthira (*Mahábharat*).
INDRASILA	The Giryek hill to the north-east of Gaya. This was famous among the Buddhists as the spot where Sákya is said to have propounded the greater part of Prajná-Parámita.

ANCIENT NAMES.		MODERN NAMES OR SITUATION.
IRÁVATI	..	The Rávi (Hydraotes of the Greeks).
ISALIA	...	Kesariya, thirty miles north of Besarh.

J

JAHNU-ÁSRAMA		The hermitage of Jahnu Muni is at Sultanganj (E. I. Railway) on the west of Bhagalpur. The temple of Gaibináth Mahádeo, which is on the site of the hermitage of Jahnu Muni, is situated on a rock which comes out from the bed of the Ganges. The river (Gangá) on her way to the ocean, was gulped down at a draught by the Muni when interrupted in his meditation by the rush of the waters, and he again let her out by making an incision in his thigh when interceded by Bhagiratha: hence the Ganges is called Jáhnavi. It is the Zanghera of Martin *(Indian Empire)*
JAJÁTIPURA	...	Jajpur (see *Yajnapura.*)
JAMADAGNI-ÁSRAMA	...	Zamánia, in the district of Ghazipur: the hermitage of Rishi Jamadagni.
JAMBUDWIPA	...	India.
JANASTHÁNA	...	Aurangabad.
JÁVALI-PATTANA		Jabbalpur.
JETAVANA-VIHÁRA	...	Joginibhariya mound, one mile to the south of Srávasti. Buddha resided and preached here for some time.

ANCIENT NAMES.	MODERN NAMES OR SITUATION.
JHÁRAKHANDA	Chota Nagpur: Kokra of the Mahomedan historians.
JIRNANAGARA ...	Jooner in the district of Poonah.
JWÁLÁMUKHI ...	A celebrated place of pilgrimage near Kangra, being one of the 52 Pithas where Sati's tongue is said to have fallen. The town is thus described by W. H. Parish in *J. A. S. B.*, Vol. XVIII: "The town of Jwálámukhi is large and straggling, and is built at the base of the western slope of the Jwálámukhi or Chungar-ki-dhar. The town with the wooded slopes of Chungar forming the background, and the valley spread out before it, has a very picturesque appearance from a distance. There is nothing interesting, however, about the town, it being filthily dirty and badly built. Even the celebrated temple itself is not free from its share of all manner of filth. It possesses no architectural beauty, nor anything worthy of notice, except the natural jets of gas." The temple contains the image of Ambiká or Máteswari.

K

KABANDHA ...	Sarik-kul and Tashkurghán (Yule).
KACHCHHA ...	Kheda in Guzerát, a large town between Ahmedabad and Khambay.
KAILÁS ...	On the north of Lake Mánas-sarovar, beyond Gangri or Darchin, the mountain is situated. It is said to be the

ANCIENT NAMES.	MODERN NAMES OR SITUATION.
	abode of Mahádeva and Párvati. "In picturesque beauty," says H. Strachey, "Kailás far surpasses the big Gurla or any other of the Indian Himalaya that I have seen : it is full of majesty,—a king of mountains." Through the ravines on either side of the mountain is the passage by which the pilgrims perform their perambulation. The Kiunlun range. The Mahábhárat includes the Choor mountain between the Sutlej and Jamuná rivers in the Kailás range.
KAJINGHARA ...	Same as *Kajughira*.
KAJUGHIRA ...	Kajeri, ninety-two miles from Champá (Beal). Cunningham identifies it with Kankjol, sixty-seven miles to the east of Champá or Bhagalpur. Kajughira is a contraction of Kubjagriha.
KAKSHIVATA ..	The Rajmahal hills.
KALINDA-DESA	A mountainous country situated in the Bándara-puchchha range of the Himalaya, where the Jamuná has got its source : hence the river is called Kálindi.
KALINGA ...	A country lying on the south of Orissa and north of Drávida on the border of the sea. According to Cunningham, it was between the Godávari river on the south-west and the Gaolya branch of the Indrávati river on the north-west. Its chief towns were Manipura and Rájamahendri. At the time of the Mahábhárata, a large portion of Orissa was included in Kalinga, its northern boundary being the river Baitarani

ANCIENT NAMES.	MODERN NAMES OR SITUATION.
KALYÁNA	Kaliani in the province of Bombay. It was the capital of the Chálukyas in the sixth century. Vijnáneswara, the author of the Mitákshará, was born at this place.
KAMALÁNKA ...	Comillah : it was the capital of Tipárá in the sixth century.
KAMPILYA ..	Kampil, twenty-eight miles north-east of Fathgarh in the Farrakhabad district. It was the capital of Rájá Drupada, who was king of South Panchála, and the scene of Draupadi's *Sayambara* Drupad's palace is pointed out as the most easterly of the isolated mounds on the bank of the Bur-Gangá. A writer in the *Tattwabodhini Patriká* identified it with Doarháttá, ten miles east from the bank of the Rámgangá. But its identification with Kampil by Cunningham and Führer appears to be the more reasonable and correct.
KANAKHALA ...	Hardwar wae once called by this name. It is now a small village, two miles to the east of Hardwar (see *Máyápuri*).
KANIKSHAPURA	Kanikhpur or Kámpur, ten miles to the south of Srinagar. It was founded by Kaniksha, king of Kásmir, who in 78 A. D. convened the last Buddhist synod, which gave rise to the Saka era.
KANSÁVATI ...	The river Kasai in Bengal.
KANWA-ÁSRAMA	Bijnor : it was the hermitage of Kanwa Muni, who adopted the celebrated Sakuntalá as his daughter.
KNYÁ-TIRTHA ...	In Kurukshetra.

ANCIENT NAMES.	MODERN NAMES OR SITUATION.
KAPILADHÁRÁ ...	1. Twenty-four miles to the south-west of Nasik: it was the hermitage of Kapila. 2. The first fall of the river Nerbuda from the Amarakantaka mountains.
KAPILAVASTU	The birth-place of Buddha. It has been identified by Carlleyle with Bhuila in the north-western part of the Basti district, about twenty-five miles north-east from Fyzabad. He places the country of Kapilavastu between the Ghagra and the Gandak, from Fyzabad to the confluence of these rivers. Cunningham identifies it with Nagarkhas on the eastern bank of the Chando Tál, near a large stream named Kohána, a tributary of the Rapti, and in the northern division of Oudh beyond the Ghagra river; and he supposes that Mokson is the site of the Lumbini garden, where Buddha was born. But the question has been set at rest by the recent exploration of Dr. Führer on the suggestion of Dr. Waddell. It has been discovered that Kapilavastu lies in the immediate neighbourhood of the Nepalese village Nigliva, north of Gorakhpur, situated in the Nepalese Terai, thirty-eight miles north-west of the Uska Station of Bengal and North-Western Railway. The Lumbini garden has been identified with the village Paderia, two miles north of Bhagavanpur. The ruins of Kapilavastu lie eight miles north-west of Paderia. Buddha was born in 557 B.C., and he died in 477 B. C.

ANCIENT NAMES.	MODERN NAMES OR SITUATION.
KAPISÁ ...	1. Kushán, ten miles west of Opian, on the declivity of the Hindu Kush. Julien supposes the district to have occupied the Panjshir and Tagao valleys in the north border of Kohistan (Beal). 2. The river Suvarnarekhá in Orissa.
KAPITHA ...	Identified by Cunningham with Sankisa or Sánkásya, forty miles south-east of Atranji (see *Sánkásya*).
KAPIVATI	Bhaigu, a branch of the Ramaganga (N. C. Das).
KARAKALLA ..	Karáchi in Scind: Krokala of Megasthenes.
KARAVIRAPURA.	A town situated on the north of the Western Ghâts near Jooner, on the bank of the Vená, a branch of the Krishná, where Krishna met Parasuráma and killed its king named Srigála (*Harivansa*).
KARATOYÁ ...	A sacred river which flows through the districts of Rungpur and Dinajpur. It formed the boundary between the kingdoms of Bengal and Kamrupa at the time of the Mahábhárat (see *Sadánirá*).
KARDDAMA-ÁSARMA ...	Sitpur (Siddhapur) in Guzerát, the hermitage of Rishi Karddama and birthplace of Kapila.
KARKOTAKA-NAGARA	Karra, forty-one miles north-west of Allahabad. It is one of the 52 Pithas where Sati's hand is said to have fallen (Führer).

ANCIENT NAMES.	MODERN NAMES OR SITUATION.
KARMANÁSÁ	The cursed river, the water of which is considered by the Hindus to be polluted, being associated with the sins of Trisanku, the *protégé* of Rishi Viswámitra. The river is on the western limit of the district of Shahabad, and forms the boundary of Behar and the North-Western Provinces. It issues from a spring situated in a village called Sarodak (Hunter's *Statistical Account of Bengal*, Vol. XII, p. 164).
KARNAPURA	Bhagalpur.
KARNA-SUVARNA	Kánsoná, in the district of Murshidabad, the former capital of Bengal at the time of Ádisura, who was identical with Vijaya Sena of the inscriptions. It was at the request of Ádisura that Bira Sinha, king of Kanouj, sent five Bráhmans, Bhattanáráyana and others, to Bengal in the latter part of the tenth century to perform his sacrifice according to the Vedas. Bhattanáráyana, the author of the drama *Veni-Samhára*, is considered by some to have flourished in the court of Dharma Pála of the Pála dynasty. Even the name of Kánsoná has become antiquated, and the town is now known by the name of Rángámáti. It is situated on the right bank of the Bhágirathi, four miles below Berhampur. Captain Laird says that Rángámáti was anciently called Kánsonápuri, and the remains of the greater part of the palace with its gate and towers are distinctly traceable, although the site is now under cultivation (*J. A. S. B.*, Vol. XXII, p. 281).

ANCIENT NAMES.		MODERN NAMES OR SITUATION.
KARNAVATI	...	The river Kane in Bundelkhand.
KARNÁTA	...	Part of the Carnatic between Ramnad and Seringapatam.
KARUSHA	...	The eastern portion of the district of Shahabad in the province of Behar.
KATADWIPA	...	Kátwa in the district of Burdwan in Bengal (Wilford).
KATRIPURA	...	Tripurá or Tipárá (Prinsep).
KAUSÁMBI	....	Kosambi-nagar or Kosám, an old village on the Jamuna, about thirty miles to the west of Allahabad. It was the capital of Vatsyadesa, the kingdom of Udayana, whose history has been given in the Vrihat Kathá and Kathásarit-ságara. Udayana was a contemporary of Buddha. The *Ratnávali*, a drama by Harsha Deva, places its scene at Kau-sámbi.
KAUSIKI	....	The river Kusi.
KAUSIKI-KACHCHHA	....	The district of Purnea.
KAUSIKI-SANGAMA	....	The confluence of the Kusi and the Ganges.
KÁLÁDI	....	In Kerala, where, according to the *Sankaravijaya*, Sankaráchárya was born in the fifth century of the Christian era ; but according to the *Sankara-Digvijaya*, he was born at Chidambar in South Arcot.

ANCIENT NAMES.	MODERN NAMES OR SITUATION.
KÁLIGHÁT ...	Near Calcutta. It is one of the 52 Pithas, where the four toes of Sati's right foot are said to have fallen. The name of Calcutta is derived from Kálighát.
KÁLINDI ...	The river Jamuna.
KÁMA-ÁSRAMA	Káron, eight miles to the north of Korantedi in the district of Balia. Mahádeva is said to have destroyed Madana, the god of Love, at this place with the fire of his third eye in the forehead (*Rámáyana*). It was situated at the confluence of the Saraju (Ghágra) and the Ganges, but the Saraju has now receded far to the east of this place, and joins the Ganges near Revel-ganj in Saran. The place contains a temple of Kámeswarnáth or Kauleswaranáth Mahádeo.
KÁMARUPA ...	1. It extended from the Karatoya river to the eastward, and included Manipur, Jayntiya, Kachhar, West Assam, and parts of Mymensingh and Sylhet. The modern district extends from Goalpara to Gauhatti. Its capital is called in the *Puráns* Prágjyotisha (Wilson). Assam 2. Kámakhyá: it is one of the 52 Pithas containing the temple of the celebrated Kámakhyá Devi.
KÁMBOJA	Afghanistan: Kaofu (Kambu) of Hiuen Tsiang. The name of Afghan, however, has been derived from Aswakán (McCrindle).

ANCIENT NAMES.	MODERN NAMES OR SITUATION.
KÁNCHIPURA ...	Conjeveram, the capital of Dravida (Chola). The southern portion of the town is called Vishnu-Kánchi, and the northern portion is called Siva-Kánchi, inhabited by the worshippers of Vishnu and Siva, respectively. Sankaráchárya died at Kánchipura, and at Siva-Kánchi exists his tomb or *Samádhi* with his statue upon it.
KÁNTIPURI	Identified by Cunningham with Kotwal, twenty miles north of Gwalior. According to others, it is one of the ancient names of Katmandu in Nepal. But the Vishnu Purán places it on the Ganges near Allahabad.
KÁNYAKUBJA	Kanouj.
KÁRÁPATHA ...	Karabagh on the Indus. It is mentioned in the *Raghuvansa* as the place where Lakshmana's son, Chandraketu, was placed as king by his uncle Ramachandra when he made a disposition of his kingdom before his death. It is the "Carabat" of Tavernier. But the distance he gives from Candahar does not tally with its actual distance from that place (Tavernier's *Travels*, Ball's Ed., Vol. I, p. 91).
KÁRTTIKEYA-PURÁ	Baijnath or Baidyanath in the district of Kumaon.
KÁRTTIKI	The river Choya, a branch of the Saraswati.

ANCIENT NAMES.	MODERN NAMES OR SITUATION.
KÁSHTHA MANDAPA ...	Katmandu, the capital of Nepal.
KÁSI ...	Benares (see *Váránasi*). Kási was properly the name of the country, of which Benares was the capital (Fa Hian).
KÁSYAPAPURA ...	Kásmir. The hermitage of Rishi Kásyapa was on the Hari mountain, three miles from Srinagar.
KEDÁRA	The temple of the Mahadeo Kedáranátha is built on a ridge jutting out at right angles from the snowy range of the Rudra-Himalaya below the peak of Mahápantha. A sacred stream called Káli-Ganga has its rise here, and it joins the Alakánandá at Rudra-Prayága. It requires eight days to go from Kedár to Badrinath, although the distance is short as the crow flies. The worship of Kedáranátha is said to have been established by the Pándavas (see *Pancha-Kedára*).
KEKAYA	A country between the Beas and the Sutlej. It was the kingdom of the father of Kaikeyi, one of the wives of Dasaratha, king of Ayodhyá.
KERALA	The Malabar coast. It comprised Malabar, Travancore and Kanara.
KESAVATI ...	The Vishnumáli river in Nepal. It forms four, out of the fourteen, great Tirthas of Nepal by its junction with four rivers. The names of the four Tirthas are Káma, Nirmala, Akara and Júgana.

ANCIENT NAMES.		MODERN NAMES OR SITUATION.
KHARKI	....	Aurangabad.
KHÁNDAVA-PRASTHA	...	Same as *Indraprastha* : Old Delhi.
KHÁNDAVA-VANA		Mozuffarnagar, north of Mirat. It is one of the stations of the North-Western Railway. Arjuna, one of the Pándavas, appeased the hunger of Agni, the god of Fire, at this place.
KHIRAGRÁMA	...	Twenty miles north of Burdwan. It is one of the 52 Pithas, where a toe of Sati's right foot is said to have fallen.
KIKATA	....	Magadha.
KIMMRITYA	....	The Kaimur range, between the rivers Sone and Tonse, being part of the Vindhya hills.
KIRANA-SUVARNA	....	Singhbhum in Chota-Nagpur (Cunningham). It was the southern part of the ancient kingdom of Magadha.
KIRÁTA-DESA	....	Tipárá. The temple of Tripureswari at Udaipur in Hill Tipárá is one of the 52 Pithas.
KISKINDHYÁ	....	"About a mile easterly from Nimbapur, a small hamlet in the suburb of Bijanugger, lies an oval-shaped heap of calcareous scoria, partially covered by grass and other vegetation. The Brahmins a er it to be the ashes of the bones of the giant Walli or Báli, an impious tyrant slain here by Ráma

F

ANCIENT NAMES. MODERN NAMES OR SITUATION.

on his expedition to Lanka (Ceylon)" *J. A. S. B.*, Vol. XIV., p. 519. But this does not correctly identify the place. From the accounts of pilgrims, it appears that the ancient Kiskindhyá is still called by that name. It is a small hamlet situated on the north bank of the river Tungabhadra near Anagandi, about sixty miles to the north of Bellary (Balhari). About two miles to the south-west of Kiskindhyá is the Pampá-sarovara, and to the north-west of Pampá-sarovara is the Anjaná hill, where Hanumána was born. Ráma killed Báli, the brother of Sugriva, and gave the kingdom of Kiskindhyá to the latter.

KLISOBORAS (OF THE GREEKS) ... Growse identifies it with Mahában, six miles to the south of Mathura on the opposite bank of the Jamuna (*Mathura*, p. 279).

KODANGALURA ... Cranganore, a town of Malabar.

KOIL .... Aligarh.

KOLÁCHALA ... The Brahmajoni range in Gaya (*Vàyu Puràn*).

KOLÁHALA-PARVATA ... The range of hills near Chanderi, which separates Malwa from Bundelkhand (*Mahábhárat*).

KOLUKA ... Same as *Kuluta*.

ANCIENT NAMES.	MODERN NAMES OR SITUATION.
KORUR ...	Between Multan and Loni, where the celebrated Vikramáditya, king of Ougein, completely defeated the Sakas in a decisive battle in 533 A. D.,—the date of this battle is supposed to have given rise to the Samvat era. It is also written Kahror.
KOSALA ...	Oudh (see *Ayodhyá*).
KOSALA (DAKSHINA) ...	Gondwana. Its capital was Ratanpur in the eleventh or twelfth century. Its former capital was Chiráyu (see *Kathásaritságara*, in which the story of Nágárjuna and King Sadvaha, called also Chirayu, is given. Comp. Hiuen Tsiang). Vidarbha or Berar in the Buddhist period was called Dakshina Kosala (Cunningham's *Geography of Ancient India*).
KOTA-TIRTHA ...	A tank situated in Kálinjár.
KOTI-TIRTHA ...	1. In Mathura. 2. A sacred tank in Gokarna.
KRATHAKAISIKA.	Same as *Payoshni*: the river Purná in Berar.
KRISHNAVENI ...	The river Krishna.
KRITAMÁLA ...	The river Vaiga, on which Madura (Dakshina-Mathurá) is situated; it has got its source in the Malaya mountain. (*Chaitanya-Charitámrita*, *Márkandeya Purán* and *Vishnu Purán*).
KRIYANA ...	The Kane river in Bundelkhand.

ANCIENT NAMES.	MODERN NAMES OR SITUATION.
KUBHÁ ...	1. The Kábul river, the Kophen of the Greeks. 2 The district through which the Kophes or Kábul river flows. The name of Kábul is derived from the Vedic name of Kubhá (Beal's *Fa Hian*).
KUBJAGRIHA ...	Same as *Kajughira*.
KUKKUTAPÁDA-GIRI ..	Kurkihar, about three miles north-east of Wazirganj, which is fifteen miles east of Gaya (Grierson's *Notes on the District of Gaya*). The three hills situated about half a mile to the north of Kurkihar are said to have been the scene of some of the miracles of the Buddhist saint Mahá-Kasyapa and eventually of his death.
KULINDA-DESA	The district of Shaharanpur, north of Delhi.
KULUTA ...	The district of Kulu in the upper valley of the Beas river. Its capital was Nagarkot.
KUMÁRASWÁMI.	This is a celebrated place of pilgrimage. The temple of Kumáraswámi or Kárttikaswami is one hundred and twenty miles to the south-east of Tripati in the province of Madras. It was visited by Sankaráchárya (*Sankaravijaya*).
KUMÁRI ...	Cape Comorin.
KUNDINAPURA ...	The ancient capital of Vidarbha. Dowson identifies it with Kundapura, about forty miles east of Amaravati (*Classical Dic.*, p. 355). It existed at the time of Bhavabhuti (*Málati-Mádhava*).

ANCIENT NAMES.	MODERN NAMES OR SITUATION.
	It was the birth-place of Rukmini, wife of Krishna. It has been identified with Kondavir in Berar (Dr. Führer's *Monumental Antiquities and Inscriptions*). Kundinapura was also called Vidarbhapura (*Harivansa*).
KUNTALA-DESA	The ancient name of the province in which Curugode is situated: part of the Bellari district.
KUNTI-BHOJA ...	An ancient town of Malwa, the birth-place of Kunti, the mother of Yudhishthira and his brothers. It was situated on the bank of a small river called Aswanadi or Aswarathanadi, which falls into the river Chambal (R. K. Roy's *Mahábhárata*).
KURUJÁNGALA	A forest country situated in Sirhind, north-west of Hastinapura. It was called Srikantha-desa during the Buddhist period; its capital was Bilaspur. It was included in Kurukshetra.
KURUKSHETRA...	Thaneswar. The district formerly included Sonepat, Amin and Panipat. The war between the Kurus and the Pándavas took place not only at Thaneswar, but also in the country around it. The Dwaipáyana-Hrada is situated at Thaneswar. At Amin, Abhimanyu, the son of Arjuna, was killed, and Aswathamá was defeated by Arjuna and his skull was severed. Amin, according to Cunningham, is the contraction of Abhimanyu-khera. Sonepat and Panipat are the corruptions of

ANCIENT NAMES.	MODERN NAMES OR SITUATION.
	Sonaprastha and Pániprastha, which were two of the five villages demanded by Yudhishthira from Durjodhana. Kurukshetra was also called Sthánu-tirtha and Samantapanchaka.
KUSABHAVANA-PURA ...	Sultanpur on the Gumti in Oudh (Thornton). It was visited by Hiuen Tsiang.
KUSAPURA ...	Same as *Kusabhavanapura* (Cunningham).
KUSÁGÁRAPURA	Rajgir, the ancient capital of Magadha. Same as *Girivrajapura.*
KUSASTHALA ...	Kanouj.
KUSASTHALI ...	Dwáraká, the capital of Krishna, in Guzerát.
KUSRVÁNA-HRADA ...	The lake Rawan-hrad.
KUSÁVATI ...	1. Dwáraká in Guzerát (Tod). It was founded by Ánartta, the nephew of Ikshaku. 2. Kasur in the Panjab, thirty-two miles to the south-east of Lahore.
KUSINAGARA ...	The place where Buddha died in 477 B. C., at the age of eighty. It has been identified by Cunningham with the present village of Kasia, thirty-five miles to the east of Gorakhpur. The charcoal ashes of Buddha's funeral pyre were enshrined in a stupa at Barhi, now called Moriyanagara in the Nyagrodha forest, visited by Hiuen Tsiang.

ANCIENT NAMES.	MODERN NAMES OR SITUATION.
KUSUMAPURA ...	1. Pátaliputra. 2. Kányakubja.
KUTIKÁ ...	The Kosila, the eastern tributary of the river Rámagangá in Oudh (N. C. Das).
KUTIKOSHTIKÁ	The Koh, a small affluent of the Rámagangá in Oudh (N. C. Das).

L

LÁKSHMANÁVATI ...	Laknauti is the corruption of Lákshmanávati. It was another name of Gour, the ruins of which lie near Malda. Hunter considers that the name of Gour was more applicable to the kingdom than to the city (*Stat. Acct. of Bengal*, Vol. VII, p. 51).
LAMPÁKÁ ...	Lamghan, on the northern bank of the Kábul river.
LANKÁ ...	1. Ceylon 2. A mountain on the south-east corner of Ceylon : it is described as three-peaked in the Rámáyana : it was the abode of Rávana (Beal). There is a place called Nikumbhilá, about forty miles from Colombo, where Indrajita performed his sacrifice (Buddhist Text Society's *Journal*, Vol. III, Pt. I, Ap.).
LAVAPURA	Called also Lavakota or Lavavára, Lahore, founded by Lava, the son of Rámachandra. The ruins of the ancient city still exist near the present city of Lahore.

ANCIENT NAMES.		MODERN NAMES OR SITUATION.
LÁNGULI	....	The river Looni in Rajputana.
LÁTA	....	Guzerát. A writer in the *Sádhaná* identifies it with a portion of the kingdom of Kanouj. It was also called Lára.
LILÁJAN	....	The river Phalgu; but, in fact, the western branch of the river Phalgu, which joins the Moháná few miles above Gaya, is called by that name.
LOHA	...	Afghanistan (*Mahábhárat*).
LOHITYA	...	1. The river Brahmaputra. 2. A portion of the river Brahmaputra is called by this name. Parasurama's axe fell from his hand when he bathed in this river, the axe having got fixed to his hand owing to the sin of killing his mother.
LOMASA-ÁSRAMA		The Lomasgir-hill, four miles north-east of Rajauli in the subdivision of Nowadah, in the district of Gaya: it was the hermitage of Lomasa Rishi (Grierson)

M

MACHHERI	...	Alwar, which formerly appertained to the territory of Jeypore (see *Matsya-desa*).
MADHUMATI	...	The Mohwar or Modhwar river which rises near Ranod and falls into the Sindh, about eight miles above Sonari in Malwa (*Málati-Mádhava*, Act IX).

ANCIENT NAMES.	MODERN NAMES OR SITUATION.
MADHUPURI ...	Mathura: it was founded by Satrughana, the youngest brother of Ráma, by killing the Rákshasa Lavana, son of Madhu. The town of the demon Madhu has been identified by Growse with Maholi, five miles to the south-west of the present town of Mathura. In Maholi is situated Madhu-vana (or forest of Madhu), a place of pilgrimage.
MADHYADESA ..	The country between Thaneswara and Allahabad.
MADHYÁRJUNA	Sixteen miles west of Tranquebar.
MADRA ...	A country in the Panjab between the Ravi and the Chenab. Its capital was Sákala. Madra was the kingdom of Rájá Salya of the Mahábhárat. Some suppose that Madra was also called Bálhika.
MAGADHA ...	The province of Behar. Its western boundary was the river Sone. The ancient capital of Magadha was Girivrajapura (modern Rajgir) at the time of Jarásandha, who was killed by Bhima, one of the five Pándavas. The capital was subsequently removed to Pátaliputra, which was formerly an insignificant village called by the name of Pátaligráma, enlarged and strengthened by Ajátasatru, king of Magadha and contemporary of Buddha, to repel the advance of the Vrijjis of Vaisali. Udayáswa, the grandson of Ajátasatru, is said to have removed his capital from Rajgriha to Pátaliputra

ANCIENT NAMES.	MODERN NAMES OR SITUATION.
	(*Váyu Purán*). At one period, the country of Magadha extended south of the Ganges from Benares to Monghir, and southwards as far as Singbhum (Hunter's *Statistical Account of Bengal*, Vol. XII, p. 65). The people of the neighbouring districts still call the districts of Patna and Gaya by the name of Magá, which is a corruption of Magadha.
MAHÁKAUSIKA	It is formed by the seven Kosis of Nepal, which are the Milamchi, the Sun Kosi or the Bhotea Kosi, the Tamba Kosi, the Likhu Kosi, the Dud Kosi, the Arun and the Tamor. The union of the Tamor, the Arun and the Sun Kosi forms the Triveni, a holy place of pilgrimage. The Triveni is immediately above Baráha. Kshetra in Purnea above Náthpur, as the point where or close to which the united Kosis issue into the plains.
MAHÁNADI ...	1. The Phalgu river in the district of Gayá. 2. A river in Orissa.
MAHÁSÁRA	Masár, a village six miles to the west of Arrah, visited by Hiuen Tsiang in the seventh century.
MAHENDRA ...	1. The Mahendra Mali hills in Ganjam and the Eastern Ghâts were known by the name of Mahendra-parvata, where Parasuráma retired after he was defeated by Ráma. The Rámáyana and the Chaitanya charitámrita apply the name specially to the Eastern Ghâts. 2. Mahi on the Malabar coast.

ANCIENT NAMES.		MODERN NAMES OR SITUATION.
MAHESWARA	...	Mysore.
MAHÍ	...	The river Mahi in Malwa.
MAHODADHI	...	The Bay of Bengal (*Raghuvansa*).
MAHODAYA	...	Kánouj.
MAHOTSAVA-NAGARA	...	Mahoba in Bundelkhand.
MAINÁKA-GIRI	...	The Sewalik range.
MAKULA-PARVATA	...	The Kaluhá-páhár, which is about twenty-six miles to the south of Buddha-Gayá and about sixteen miles to the north of Chátrá in the district of Hazaribagh, is evidently a corruption of the name of the Makula Parvata of the Burmese annals of Buddhism (see Bigandet's *Life or Legend of Gaudama*). Buddha is said to have passed his sixth Wasso (or rainy-season retirement) on the Makula mountain. It forms the western boundary of a secluded valley on the eastern bank of the Lilájan river, containing a temple of Durgá called Kuleswari (Kula and Iswari). But the place abounds with Buddhist architectural remains and figures of Buddha. On a plateau just in front of the hill on which Kuleswari's temple is situated, and on the eastern side of a ravine which separates the plateau from the hill, is a temple which contains a broken image of Buddha in the conventional form of meditation. There are also two impressions of Buddha's feet on the top of the highest peak

ANCIENT NAMES. MODERN NAMES OR SITUATION.

of a hill on the northern side of the valley called the *Ákásalochana*, and figures of Buddha carved in the central part of the hill with inscriptions which have become much obliterated by time and exposure. The large bricks found at this hill also attest to the antiquity of the place. The letter, "Ma" of *Makula* must have dropped down by lapse of time, and *kula* was corrupted into *kaluha*. There can be no doubt that the Brahmins appropriated this sacred place of the Buddhists and set up the image of Durgá at a subsequent period after the expulsion of Buddhism.

MALADA ... The western portion of the district of Shahabad.

MALAYA-GIRI ... The southern part of the Western Ghâts, south of the river Kaveri (Bhavabhuti's *Mahávira-charita*).

MALAYÁLAM ... Malábar.

MALLA-DESA ... 1. The district of Multan was the ancient Malla-desa, the people of which were called Mallis by Alexander's historians. Its capital was Multan (Cunningham). Lakshman's son, Angada, was made king of Malla-desa by his uncle Rámachandra. 2. The country in which the Párasnáth hills are situated (Yule), that is, portions of the districts of Hazaribagh and Manbhum. The Puráns mention two countries by the name Malla, one in the west and the other in the east.

ANCIENT NAMES.	MODERN NAMES OR SITUATION.
MALLA-PARVATA	The Párasnáth hill in Chhota-Nagpur, the Mount Maleus of the Greeks (Yule). See *Samet-sekhara.*
MALLÁRA ...	It is a contraction of Malabar.
MANDÁKINI ...	1. The Kali-gangá, which rises in the mountains of Kedár. 2. The Paisuni (Payaswini) in Bundelkhand, which flows by the side of Mount Chitrakuta.
MANDÁRA-GIRI...	A hill situated in the Banka subdivision of the district of Bhágalpur, two or three miles from Bansi. It contains a groove around it in the middle. The gods are said to have churned the ocean with this hill as a churner. There are two temples on the top of the hill, one containing representations of six human feet, and the other contained an image of Vishnu called Madhusudana, but it is now empty. There are extensive ruins scattered about the foot of the hill for above two miles, of the time of the Chole Rájás, especially of Rájá Chatra Singh, who lived before the time of the Mahomedans (Martin's *Eastern India*, Vol. II). For its sanctity see *Skanda Purán.*
MANGALA ...	Called also Mangali, the capital of Udyána, identified by Cunningham with Mangora or Manglora.
MANGIPATTANA	Balabhi or Dhank, the ancient capital of Sauráshtra or Guzerát, ten miles northwest of Bhaonagar. It was destroyed in the sixth century at the time of Siláditya (Tod).

ANCIENT NAMES.	MODERN NAMES OR SITUATION.
MANIPURA ...	It was the capital of Kalinga, the kingdom of Bubruváhana of the Mahábhárat. R. K. Roy in his *Mahábhárat* (*Aswamedha Parva*), places it to the south of Chikakole. But the situation of the capital of Kalinga, as described in the Mahábhárat and the Raghuvansa, and also the name, accord with those of Mánikapattana, a seaport at the mouth of the Chilka lake.
MARUDBRIDDHA	The Rávi.
MARUSTHALI ...	The great desert east of Sindh.
MATHURA ...	1. The capital of Surasena. It was the birth-place of Krishna. At a place called *Janma-bhumi* or *Káràgárh* on the margin of the Potara-kund tank near the temple of Kesava Deva, he was born; in the adjoining suburb called Malla-pura, he fought with the two wrestlers, Chánura and Mushtika; at Kubjá's well he cured Kubjá of her hump; at *Kansa-ka-Tilá* outside the south gate of the present city, he killed Kansa; and at *Bisráma Ghát* he rested himself after his victory. The *Jog-ghát* marks the spot where Kansa is said to have dashed Máyá or Joganidrá to the ground. Mathura was the hermitage of Dhruva: near *Dhruva-ghát* there is a temple dedicated to him. Growse identifies the *Kankáli Tilá* near the Kátra with the monastery of Upagupta visited by Hiuen Tsiang, the temple of Bhuteswara with the stupa of Sáriputra, the Jamalpur mound with the monkey-stupa, and the Yasa Vihára

ANCIENT NAMES.	MODERN NAMES OR SITUATION.
	with the temple of Kesava Deva which has been graphically described by Tavernier as the temple of "Rám Rám" before its destruction by Aurangzebe in 1669. Mathura was also called Madhupuri (present Maholi, five miles to the south-west of the modern city), the abode of Madhu, whose son Lavana was killed by Satrughana, the brother of Rámachandra, who founded the present city (Growse's *Mathura*). 2. Madura, the capital of Pándya, in the province of Madras: it is said to have been founded by Kula Sekhara. It was called Dakshina-Mathura by way of contradistinction to Mathura of the N. W. Provinces.
MATIPURA ...	Madáwar or Mundore in Western Rohilkhand, eight miles north of Bijnor.
MATSYA-DESA ...	The country around Jeypur. It was the kingdom of Rájá Viráta of the Mahábhárata, in whose court at Vairát Yudhishthira and his brothers resided *incognito* for one year during the last year of their banishment. Váirát or Bairát is in the Alwar state of Rajputana. Machheri, which is a corruption of Matsya, is the present town of Alwar, which formerly appertained to the territory of Jeypur.
MAULI ...	The Rohtas hills.
MAYA-RÁSHTRA	Mirát, where the remnant of Maya Dánava's fort is still pointed out in a place called Andha Kota. The Bille-

ANCIENT NAMES.		MODERN NAMES OR SITUATION.
		swara Mahadeo there is said to have been worshipped by Mandodari, the wife of Rávana and daughter of Maya Dánava.
MAYARÁT	...	Same as *Maya-ráshtra.*
MAYURA	...	Máyápuri or Hardwar. The present Máyápuri is situated between the town of Hardwar and Kankhala.
MÁHISHAKA	...	Mysore.
MÁHISMATI	...	Maheswara or Mahes on the right bank of the Nerbuda, forty miles to the south of Indore. It was the capital of Haihaya or Anupadesa, the kingdom of the myriad-handed Kártya-vyárjuna of the Puráns.
MÁLAVA	...	Malwa, its capital was Dhárá-nagara at the time of Rájá Bhoja. (See *Avanti*).
MÁLINI	...	1. Champánagar near Bhágalpur. 2. The river Mandákini (*Prakriti-váda*). 3 The river Málini flows between the countries called Pralamba on the west and Apartala on the east, and falls into the river Ghagra about fifty miles above Ajodhyá. It is the Erineses of Megasthenes The hermitage of Kanwa, the adoptive father of the celebrated Sakuntalá, was situated on the bank of this river. Griffith says its present name is Chuka, a branch of the Saraju.
MÁLYAVÁNA-GIRI		The Eastern Gháts.

ANCIENT NAMES.	MODERN NAMES OR SITUATION.
MÁNASA ...	Lake Manasarovar, situated in Undes or Hundesa. It has been graphically described by Moorcroft in the *Asiatic Researches*, Vol. XII, p. 375. According to his estimate, it is fifteen miles in length (east to west) by eleven miles in breadth (north to south). It cannot be marched round in less than twenty-five days.
MÁNIKAPURA ...	Manikalya in the Punjab, celebrated for the Buddhist topes, where Buddha in a former birth gave his body to feed a starving tiger.
MÁNYAKSHETRA	Malkhead on the river Krishna.
MÁRKANDA-ÁSRAMA ...	At the confluence of the Saraju and the Gomati near Bágeswara in the district of Kumanu. Márkanda Rishi performed asceticism at this place.
MÁYÁPURI ..	It included Hardwar, Máyápur and Kankhala. Kankhala is two miles from Hardwar: it was here that the celebrated *Daksha-yajna* of the Puráns took place, and Sati, the daughter of Daksha, sacrificed her life, unable to bear the insult put upon her husband Mahádeva by her father. The present Máyápur is situated between Hardwar and Kankhala. Pilgrims from all parts of India go to bathe at the Brahmakunda in the *ghát* called Har-ki-pairi at Hardwar. In a temple behind the temple of Daksheswara Mahádeo at Kankhala, the *Yajna-Kunda*, where Sati immolated herself, is still pointed out.

ANCIENT NAMES.	MODERN NAMES OR SITUATION.
	At the time of the Skanda Purán and Kálidás, Hardwar was known by the name of Kankhala.
MEDHÁVI-TIRTHA ...	Near Mount Kálinjar in Bundelkhand.
MEGNÁDA ...	The river Megná.
MEGHAVÁHANA	The river Megná.
MEKALA ...	The Mount Amarakantaka, in which the river Nerbudá has got its source: hence the Nerbudá is called Mekala-kanyaká (*Amarakosha*).
MINÁKSHI ...	Madura, one of the 52 Pithas where Sati's eyes are said to have fallen. The temple of Minákshi Devi is situated within the town: it is said to have been built by Viswanath, the first king of the Nyak dynasty, in 1520 A.D. (Fergusson).
MITHILÁ ...	1 Tirhut, 2 Janakpur (see *Videha*).
MODÁGIRI ...	Monghir (*Mahâbhárat*).
MOHANA ...	The southern portion of the Circars.
MRIGADÁVA ...	Sárnáth, six miles from Benares, the place where Buddha preached his first sermon after the attainment of Buddha-hood at Buddha-Gayá.
MUCHKUNDA	A lake three miles to the west of Dhol-pur where Kála-yavana, an ally of Jará-sandha, was by the device of Krishna consumed with a glance by Muchkunda when he was rudely awaken from his

ANCIENT NAMES.	MODERN NAMES OR SITUATION.
	slumber (Growse's *Mathura*, p. 65). On the site of the lake there was formerly a mountain.
MUDGA-GIRI ...	Monghir (see *Mudgala-giri*).
MUDGALA-GIRI	Monghir. Mudgalaputra, a disciple of Buddha, converted Srutavinsatikoti, a rich merchant of this place, into Buddhism. The *Kashtaharini Ghát* at Monghir derives its sanctity from Ráma having bathed in this ghát to expiate his sin for having killed Rávana, who, though a *rákshasa*, was nevertheless a Bráhman (*Kurma Puran*). Rámachandra is also said to have expiated his sin of slaying Rávana by bathing at a sacred tank at Hattia Haran, twenty-eight miles south-east of Hardoi in Oudh, and also in the river Gumti at Dhopáp, eighteen miles south-east of Sultanpur in Oudh (Führer).
MUKTAVENI ...	Triveni, north of Hugli. Muktaveni is used by way of contradistinction to Yuktaveni or Allahabad, where the three rivers Gangá, Jamuná, and Saraswati unite and flow together ; at Muktaveni the three rivers separate and flow in different directions.
MUKTINÁTHA ...	A celebrated temple of Náráyana situated in Thibet in the Sapta Gandaki range of the Himalaya, not far from the source of the Gandak.
MULASTHÁNA-PURA ...	Multan. Vishnu incarnated in this place as Nrisinha-Avatára, and killed the *Asura* Hiranyakasipu, the father of

ANCIENT NAMES.	MODERN NAMES OR SITUATION
	Prahláda. The temple of Nrisinha Deva is still called Prahládapuri (Cunningham's *Geography of Ancient India*) The temple of the Sun is said to have been built by Sámba, the son of Krishna, who was cured here of his leprosy by the god (*Bhavishya Purán*). It was the capital of Malla-desa or the country of the Mallis of Alexander's historians.
MURALÁ ...	The river Nerbuda.
MURANDÁ ...	Same as *Lampáká*.

N

NAGARAHÁRA ..	The town was situated at the confluence of the Surkhar or Surkh-rud and Kábul rivers, near Jalalabad.
NAGARAKOTA	Kangra, where the temple of Bajreswari is situated. It was the old capital of Kuluta.
NAIMISHÁRANYA	Nimkháravana or Nimsar, twenty-four miles from the Sandila station of the Oudh and Rohilkhand Railway, and twenty miles from Sitapur. It was the abode of sixty thousand Rishis. Many of the Puráns were written perhaps at this place. It is situated on the left bank of the Gumti.
NAIRANJANA	The river Phalgu. Its two branches are the Nilájan and the Mohána, and their united stream is called the Phalgu. Buddha-Gayá is situated at a short dis-

ANCIENT NAMES.	MODERN NAMES OR SITUATION.
	tance to the west of the Nilájana or Niranjan, which has got its source near Simeria in the district of Hazaribagh.
NANDÁ ...	The river Panchána or Panchánana which flows through the districts of Gayá and Patna. It flows by the side of Ratnagiri, called Hemakuta or Rishabha-giri, one of the five hills of Rajgir, where Rishabha Rishi performed asceticism. Rishabha Rishi's image is sculptured in the Baibhára-giri near the Sonebhándár cave.
NANDIGRÁMA ...	Nundgáon in Oudh (*Rámáyana*).
NARMADÁ ...	The river Nerbuda. It rises in the Amarakantaka mountain.
NAVADEVAKULA	Nawal, thirty-three miles north-west of Unao near Bángarmau in Oudh, visited by Hiuen Tsiang.
NAVADWIPA ...	The birth-place of Chaitanya, the great religious reformer of Bengal. The Navadwipa of Chaitanya was situated opposite to the present Navadwipa across the river Ganges: the present Navadwipa is situated on the site of the ancient village of Kulia (*Amiya Nemái Charita*). Chaitanya was born in 1485 and he died in 1527.
NÁGA-HRADA ...	The Sárik-Kul lake,—the lake of the Great Pamir (Beal).
NÁLANDA ...	Baragaon, which lies seven miles north of Rajgir, in the district of Patna, once the celebrated seat of Buddhist learning

ANCIENT NAMES.	MODERN NAMES OR SITUATION.
	(Cunningham). It was the birth-place of Sáriputra, the famous disciple of Buddha (Bigandet), but according to Hiuen Tsiang, he was born at Kálapinága. The celebrated Nágárjuna who introduced the *Maháyána* system of Buddhism in the first century, resided in the monastery of Nálanda, making it the seat of the Mahá-yána school for Central India (Fergusson).
NIKAI (of the Greeks) ...	Mong, where the celebrated battle was fought between Alexander the Great and Porus (Cunningham). Mong is now called Murg, a town in the district of Guzerat in the Panjab. Nikai is said to have been built by Alexander on the site of the field of battle.
NILANCHANA ...	Same as *Nilájana.*
NILÁJANA ...	The upper part of the river Phalgu. It is also called Lilájana.
NISHADHA ...	1. Narwar, the capital of Nala Rájá (Tod). Narwar is the contraction of Nalapura. It is situated on the right bank of the river Sindh, forty miles to the south-west of Gwaliar. 2. The mountains which lie to the north of the Kábul river, called by the Greeks Paropamisos, now called Hindu Kush (Lassen). Paropamisos or Paropanisos is evidently a contraction of Parvata Upa-Nishadha, as McCrindle says that Hindu Kush generally designates now the eastern part of the range and Paropamisos the western (McCrindle's *Ancient India*, p. 182).

ANCIENT NAMES.		MODERN NAMES OR SITUATION.
NYSA	...	Nysatta on the northern bank of the Kábul river about two leagues below Hashtnagar (St. Martin).

O

ODRA	...	Orissa.
OMKÁRANÁTHA		Same as *Amareswara*.

P

PADMAKSHETRA		Kanárak, called the Black Pagoda, nineteen miles north-west of Puri in Orissa. It contains a temple of the sun (*Surya*), said to have been established by Sámba, a son of Krishna, who was cured here of leprosy by the god. According to some account, he was cured at Multan (see *Mulasthánapura*). It appears, however, that this temple was built by Lánguliyá Narsinh, the seventh king of the Gangávansi dynasty, who reigned from 1237 to 1282 A. D. (Hunter's *Orissa*).
PADMAPURA	....	Same as *Padmávati*: it was the birth-place of Bhavabhuti.
PADMÁVATI	....	It has been identified by Cunningham with Narwar or Nalapura (*Archæological Report*, Vol. III). But this identification does not appear to be correct. The town was situated at the confluence of the rivers Sindhu (Sindh) and Párá (Párvati) in Vidarbha (*Málati-Mádhava*, Act IV), and therefore it may be

ANCIENT NAMES. MODERN NAMES OR SITUATION.

safely identified with Vijayanagar, which is a corruption of Vidyánagara, Padmávati being celebrated as a place of learning, especially for its teaching in logic, in the eighth century at the time of Bhavabhuti, who was born at this place (*Máhaviracharita* and *Málati Mádhava*).

PAMPÁ ... A branch of the river Tungabhadrá: it rises in the Rishyamukha mountain which is eight miles from the Anagandi hills, where Ráma met Hanumána and Sugriva for the first time. Near it is a lake called Pampásarovara (Wilson).

PANCHA-DRÁVIDA ... Drávida, Karnáta, Guzerát, Maháráshtra and Tailanga (Wilson).

PANCHA-GANGÁ The five Gangás are Bhágirathi (Ganges), Gomati (Godávari), Krishnaveni (Krishná), Pinákini (Pennar), and Káveri.

PANCHA-KEDÁRA The temples of Kedáranáth, Tunganáth, Rudranáth, Madhyameswara, and Kalpeswara,—all situated along the Himalayan chain,—form a peculiar object of pilgrimage, and they are collectively called Pancha-Kedára. Mahádeo, in the form of Sadásiva, fled from Arjuna, one of the five Pándavas, and took refuge at Kedáranáth in the shape of a buffalo, but finding himself hard pressed, dived into the ground, leaving his hinderparts on the surface, still an object of adoration here. The remaining portions of the god are

ANCIENT NAMES.	MODERN NAMES OR SITUATION.
	worshipped at four other places: the arms (*báhu*) at Tunganáth, the face (*mukha*) at Rudranáth, the belly (*nábhi*) at Madhyameswara, and the hair (*jatá*) and head at Kalpeswara (Führer).
PANCHA-NADA ...	The Panjab,—the country of five rivers called Satadru, Vipásá, Irávati, Chandrabhágá and Vitastá.
PANCHÁPSARÁ-TIRTHA ...	In the district of Udayapur, one of the tributary states in the Chhota-Nagpur division. Kapu, Bandhanpur, Banjiamba and Ponri are supposed to be on the site of the Pancháрsará lake of the Rámáyana.
PANCHA-PRAYÁGA ...	(1) Devaprayága at the confluence of the Bhágirathi and the Alakánandá; (2) Karnaprayága at the confluence of the Alakánandá and the Pindar river; (3) Rudraprayága at the confluence of the Alakánandá and the Káligangá (Mandákini): (4) Nandaprayága at the confluence of the Alakánandá and the Nandákini, a small river; (5) Vishunprayága at the confluence of the Alakánandá and the Dauli (Dudgangá).
PANCHA-TIRTHA	1. A collective name given to five pools, or basins of water, situated between two hills on the west of Hardwar: their names are Amrita-kunda, Tapta-kunda, Ráma-kunda, Sitá-kunda, and Surya-kunda. 2. A place of pilgrimage in the province of Madras, mentioned in the Mahàbhárat: it was visited by Arjuna.

ANCIENT NAMES.	MODERN NAMES OR SITUATION.
PANCHAVATI ...	Nasik on the Godavari, where Ráma dwelt with Lakshmana and Sitá during his exile; it was here that Sitá was abducted by Rávana, king of Lanká. The Chaitya cave at Nasik is supposed by Fergusson to belong to the second and third centuries of the Christian era.
PARASURÁMA-KSHETRA ...	Koncan (see *Surpáraka-tirtha*).
PARASURÁMA-PURA ...	Twelve miles south-east of Patti in the district of Pratapgarh in Oudh. It is one of the 52 Pithas where a portion of Sati's body is said to have fallen.
PARNÁSÁ ...	The river Banas in Rajputana: a tributary of the Chambal.
PARUSHNI ...	The river Rávi (Irávati) in the Panjab.
PARVATA ...	A country in the Panjab, between the Rávi and the Sutlej.
PASUPATINÁTHA	A celebrated temple of Mahádeo in Nepal, associated with the story of the fowler and the god: it is said that the fowler obtained the boon of salvation from Mahádeo at this place as the drippings of blood from his bag of game fell upon the head of the latter.
PATALA ...	Tatta in Sindh, mentioned in the *Periplus of the Erythrean Sea*. Cunningham identifies it with Hyderabad in Sindh.
PAYOSHNI ...	The river Purná, one of the branches of the Tapti in Berar.

ANCIENT NAMES.		MODERN NAMES OR SITUATION.
PÁNCHÁLA	...	Rohilkhand. Pánchála was divided into North and South Pánchála: the capital of the former was Ahichhatra, and the capital of the latter was Kampilya. South Pánchála was the kingdom of Rájá Drupada, whose daughter Draupadi was married to the five Pándavas.
PÁNDU	...	Same as *Pándya.*
PÁNDUPURA	...	Pánderpur on the river Bhimarathi or Bhima in the district of Sholapur in the province of Bombay. It contains the celebrated temple of Bithoba Deva or Bithalnáth, an image of Krishna. It was visited by Chaitanya.
PÁNDYA	...	The modern districts of Tinnivelly and Madura. Its capitals at different periods were Uragapura (modern Negapatam) and Mathura (modern Madura). Pandion, a king of Pándya, is said to have sent an embassy to Augustus Cæsar at Rome in 27 B. C. (Gibbon).
PÁNIPRASTHA	...	Panipat, one of the five villages demanded by Yudhishthira from Durjodhana (see *Kurukshetra*).
PÁRASYA	...	Persia: its chief town, according to Hiuen Tsiang, was Surasthána.
PÁRÁ	...	The river Párvati which, winding to the north of Narwar, falls into the Sindhu near Vijayanagar in Malwa.
PÁRÁVATI	...	Same as *Párá*

ANCIENT NAMES.	MODERN NAMES OR SITUATION.
PÁRIPÁTRA ...	The western part of the Vindhyá range extending from the source of the Nerbuda to the Gulf of Cambay. It included the Aravali mountains.
PÁRIYÁTRA ...	Same as *Páripátra*.
PÁRVATI-KSHETRA ...	Same as *Birajá*.
PÁTALÁVATI	The Kali-Scind, a branch of the Chambal, mentioned by Bhavabhuti in his Málati-Mádhava. It is called Palaitah by Tod.
PÁTALIPUTRA ...	Patna, built by Ajátasatru, king of Magadha and contemporary of Buddha, for the purpose of repelling the attacks of the Vrijjis of Vaisali (Besarh). The old capital of Magadha was Girivrajapura or Rajgir, but it was subsequently removed to Pátaliputra by Udayáswa, the grandson of Ajátasatru. A very small portion of the modern town of Patna is on the site of the ancient Pátaliputra, the greater portion of which was diluviated by the rivers Ganges and Sone in 750 A. D. It was the birthplace of Árya Bhatta, the celebrated Hindu astronomer. Several Hindu sages, as Kátyáyana and Chánakya, flourished in this place. A graphic description of the town has been given by Megasthenes, who was sent as an ambassador by Seleucus Nicator to the court of Chandragupta, king of Magadha, who reigned from 320 to 290 B. C. He

ANCIENT NAMES.		MODERN NAMES OR SITUATION.
		describes the town as being situated near the confluence of the rivers Ganges and Erannoboas (Sone), and says that it was eighty stadia in length and fifteen in breadth, and that it was surrounded by a ditch thirty cubits deep, and that the walls were adorned with 570 towers and 64 gates.
PÁVANI	...	The river Irawadi in Burma.
PERIMUDA	...	The island of Salsette near Bombay,—the Perimula of the Greeks. It derived its sanctity from a tooth of Buddha which was enshrined there at the beginning of the fourth century of the Christian era, and which was visited by Buddhist pilgrims. The Kenheri cave (Chaitya) in the island is supposed by Fergusson to belong to the early part of the fifth century of the Christian era.
PHULLAGRÁMA		Chittagong.
PINÁKINI	...	The river Pennar in the Madras presidency.
PRABHÁSA	...	Somnath in Guzerát. "The neighbourhood of Pattana" (which contains the celebrated temple of Somnath at its south-western corner) "is esteemed especially sacred by the Hindus as the scene of Krishna's death and apotheosis. A small river, known to Hindu devotees as the Raunakshi, empties itself into the sea, at the distance of about a mile to the eastward of Pattana. At a particular spot on this river, sacred as that

ANCIENT NAMES.	MODERN NAMES OR SITUATION.
	of Krishna's death, are a ghát and a few temples" (*J. A. S. B.*, Vol vii : *Notes of a Journey to Girnár*). Raunakshi is another name of the river Saraśwati. Somnáth is known to the Jains under the title of *Chandra Prabhása*. It was formerly frequented by a very large number of pilgrims from all parts of India during an eclipse of the moon. Chandra (the moon) is said to have been cured of consumption, with which he was cursed, by bathing in the river Saraswati.
PRADYUMNA-NAGARA ...	Pándua in the district of Hughli.
PRAHLÁDAPURI	Multán (see *Mulasthánapura*).
PRAJÁPATIVEDI	A sacred place in Allahabad where Brahmá performed sacrifice: this is the temple of Alopi, which is considered as one of the 52 Pithas where Sati's back is said to have fallen. The temple contains no image, but only a *Vedi*.
PRALAMBA ...	Madáwár, or Mundore, eight miles north of Bijnor in Western Rohilkhand.
PRANAHITÁ ...	The united stream of the rivers Wardhá and the Waingangá.
PRASRAVANA-GIRI ...	The hills of Arangabad situated on the banks of the Godávari, graphically described by Bhavabhuti in his Uttaracharita : in one of the peaks of these hills dwelt the bird Jatáyu of the Rámáyana.

ANCIENT NAMES.	MODERN NAMES OR SITUATION.
PRATISTHÁNA ...	1. Bithoor, where the remains of a fort, which is said to have been the fort of Rájá Uttánapáda, still exist. The celebrated Dhruva was the son of Uttánapáda: he was born at this place: he performed asceticism in the forests of Mathura. 2. There was another town of that name in the Deccan now called Pattana or Mangila-Pattana, thirty-eight miles south-west of Aurangabad: it was the capital of Rájá Sáliváhana. 3. Paithana: it was once a great emporium of commerce in the Andhra country, described by Pliny. 4. Jhusi, opposite to Allahabad, across the Ganges: it is still called Pratisthápur. It was the capital of Rájá Puraravas.
PRAYÁGA ...	Allahabad. The celebrated *Akshaya Vata* or the undecaying banyan tree, which is still an object of worship, and which is now situated within a dark subterranean chamber in the fort at Allahabad, is thus described by Hiuen Tsiang, who visited India in the seventh century: "In the city there is a Deva temple beautifully ornamented and celebrated for its numerous miracles. According to their records, this place is a noted one for all living things to acquire religious merit." He further says: "Before the hall of the temple there is a great tree with spreading boughs and branches, and casting a deep shadow. There was a body-eating demon here, who, depending on this custom (*viz., of committing*

ANCIENT NAMES.	MODERN NAMES OR SITUATION.
	suicide), made his abode here; accordingly on the left and right one sees heaps of bones. Hence, when a person comes to this temple, there is everything to persuade him to despise his life and give it up; he is encouraged thereto both by the promptings of the heretics and also by the seductions of the (evil) spirit. From very early days till now this false custom has been practised."
PRÁGJOTISHA-PURA ...	Kámrup or Kámakshyá in Assam.
PRÁGVIJAYA ...	Jyntea.
PRETODDHÁRINI	The river Pyri which joins the Mahánadi at Raju.
PRITHUDAKA ...	Pehoa, where the celebrated Brahmayoni-tirtha is situated. It is fourteen miles to the west of Thaneswara.
PULAHA-ÁSRAMA	Same as *Sálagráma*.
PULINDA-DESA.	It included the western portion of Bundelkhand and the district of Sagar.
PUNDRAVARDHANA ...	1 Pándua, called Firuzabad in later times, six miles north of Máldá (Westmacott). According to Wilson, the ancient Pundra included the districts of Rajshahi, Dinajpur, Rangpur, Nadia, Birbhoom, Midnapura, the Jangal Mahals, Pachet and part of Chunar. Mr. Westmacott also identifies it with Pánjara and Barddhankuti (or Khettál)

ANCIENT NAMES.	MODERN NAMES OR SITUATION.
	in Dinajpur. Cunningham has identified the capital with Mahásthánagarh on the Karatoyá river, twelve miles south of Barddhankuti, and also with Pabná. James Taylor in his *Remarks on the Sequel to the Periplus of the Erythrean Sea (J. A. S. B.*, Vol. XV*)* says that in the Kesava Sena Plate, found at Edilpur in the district of Bakergunge, Vikrampur is said to have been Paundraka (see a transcription of the plate in *J. A. S. B.* of 1838). 2. North Bengal.
PURÁNÁDHISTHÁNA ...	Pandritan. It was the ancient capital of Kásmir.
PURNADARBHA...	Kálinjar.
PURUSHAPURA	Peshawur, the capital of Gándhára.
PURUSHOTTAMAKSHETRA ...	Puri in Orissa (see *Srikshetra*).
PURVA-GANGÁ ...	The river Nerbudá.
PUSHKALÁVATI	Pushkalávati or Pushkarávati, the old capital of Gándhára, is said to have been founded by Pushkara or Pushkala, the son of Bharata and nephew of Ráma. Alexander the Great besieged and took it from Astes (Hasti) and placed Sangœus (Sanjaya) as his successor. It was probably Hashtanagar, eighteen miles north of Peshawur, on the Swát, near its junction with the Kabul river (Cunningham). It was the Peukelaotes of the

ANCIENT NAMES.	MODERN NAMES OR SITUATION.
	Greeks, situated on the Indus, fifteen miles north-eastward beyond the Cabul river (Lassen).
PUSHKARA ...	The Pushkar lake, six miles from Ajmir. It is called also Pokhrá.
PUSHKARÁVATI	Same as *Pushkalávati*.

R

RAGHUNANDANA	The range of hills that lies between Bengal and Tipárá.
RAIVATA ...	Mount Girnár near Junágar in Guzerát.
RAIVATAKA ...	Same as *Raivata*.
RAMANYA ...	Pegu and the delta of the Iráwadi. It was also called Aramana (Beal).
RANTIPURA ...	Rintambur on the Chambal. It was the abode of Ranti Deva alluded to by Kálidása in his Meghaduta. The story of Ranti Deva's sacrifice of cows has been given in the Mahábhárat (Wilson).
RATNVDWIPA ...	Ceylon.
RATNAPURA ...	Ratanpur, the capital of Dakshina Kosala or Gondwana.
RÁJAGRIHA ...	1. Rájgir, the ancient capital of Magadha (see *Girivrajapura*). The new town of Rájagriha was built by Bimbisára, the father of Ajátasatru, at the distance of about a mile to the north of the old town of Rájagriha or Girivrajapura of the Mahábhárat (Cunningham and Bigandet). 2. Rájagiri on the north

ANCIENT NAMES.	MODERN NAMES OR SITUATION.
	bank of the Beas in the Panjab: the capital of the Aswapatis of the Rámáyana (St. Martin).
RÁJAMAHENDRI	The capital of Kalinga, founded by Mahendra Deva.
RÀJAPURI ...	Rajauri, south of Kásmir, and south-east of Punach, called Puhats by the Kásmiris.
RÁMAGIRI ...	Rámtege (Ramtek), north of Nágpur in Central India (Wilson). Traditionally Ramtek was the place where Sambuka, a Sudra, performed asceticism, for which reason he was killed by Rámachandra. It contains a temple of Rámachandra, and also a temple dedicated to Nágárjuna. Kálidása places the scene of his story in *Meghaduta* at Rámagiri. Rámagiri has also been identified with Rámgarh in Sirguja, one of the tributary states of Chhota Nágpur. There is a large cavern called Sitá Bangira cave high up in the rocks, forty-five feet deep and six high, at the entrance, containing inscriptions of the time of Asoka. There is also a natural fissure in the mountain called Háttiphor tunnel (cave), through which a small rivulet has worn a passage. The tunnel is 450 feet long with a diameter ranging from 55 to 16 feet, and height 108 feet. This cave is noticed in the Rámáyana and in the Raghuvansa (*Archæological Survey Reports*, Vol. XIII, p. 41, and *List of Ancient Monuments in the Chota Nagpur Division*).

ANCIENT NAMES.	MODERN NAMES OR SITUATION.
RÁMA-HRADA ...	A sacred tank situated near Thaneswar, where Parasuráma is said to have given oblations to the manes of his ancestors after destroying the Kshatriyas.
RÁMESWARA-SANGAMA ...	The confluence of the river Banas with the Chambal.
RÁRA ...	That part of Bengal which lies to the west of the Ganges.
RÁVANA-HRADA	It is the Kusavána-hrada of the time of the Mahábhárat, and Anava-tapta or Anava-tatta of the Buddhist period. The lake is fifty miles in length and twenty-five miles in breadth. There is a hill in the middle of the lake. On the bank of the lake, in the Gyantang monastery, there is a gigantic image of Rávana, king of Lanká. He is said to have bathed every day in the lake, and then worshipped Mahádeva in the Kailása mountain at a place called Homa-kunda. The Sutlej is said to have its source in this lake.
RENUKÁ-TIRTHA	About sixteen miles north of Nahan in the Punjab. Renuká was the mother of Parasuráma.
REVÁ ...	The river Nerbudá.
RIKSHA-PARVATA	The eastern part of the Vindhyá range extending from the Bay of Bengal to the source of the Nerbudá. The mountains of Gondwana.

ANCIENT NAMES.	MODERN NAMES OR SITUATION.
RISHABHA-PARVATA ...	1. The Palni hills in Madura. 2. The Ratna-giri hill, called also Hemakuta in the Mahábhárat, one of the five hills of Rájgir (see *Nanda*).
RISHIKULYÁ ...	The Rishikuilia river on which Ganjam is situated: it rises in the Mahendra hills.
RISHIPATTANA...	Sárnáth near Benares: Isipatana of the Buddhists.
RISHYAMUKHA...	A mountain situated eight miles from Anagandi on the bank of the Tungabhadra. The river Pampá rises in this mountain and falls into the Tungabhadra after flowing westward. It was at this mountain that Rámachandra met Hanumána and Sugriva for the first time (*Rámáyana* and P. N. Ghosal's *Travels*).
RISHYASRINGA-ÁSRAMA ...	The hermitage of Rishi Rishyasringa of the Rámáyana was situated at Singheswara in the sub-division of Madhipura, district Bhagalpur. Singheswara is the corruption of Rishyasringa. Bibhándaka was the father of Rishyasringa.
ROHANA ...	Adam's Peak in Ceylon: it was also called Sumana-kuta.
ROHI ...	Afghanistan: it was also called Roha. Same as *Loha*.
ROHITA ...	Rohtas in the district of Shahabad in Bengal, celebrated for its fort, which is said to have been built by Rohitáswa, son of Rájá Harisachandra of the Rámáyana and Márkandeya Purán.

ANCIENT NAMES.	MODERN NAMES OR SITUATION.
ROHITAKA ...	Rohtak, forty-two miles norh-west of Delhi.

S

SADÁNIRÁ ...	1. The river Karatoyá which flows through the districts of Rungpur and Dinajpur. The river is said to have been formed by the perspiration which flowed from the hand of Siva at the time of his marriage with Durgá. 2. A river in Oudh mentioned in the Mahábhárat and Satapatha Brahmana.
SAHANSARÁMA ...	Sásirám in the district of Shahabad (Edicts of Asoka who reigned from 276 to 240 B. C.)
SAHYÁDRI ...	The northern part of the Western Gháts north of the river Káveri.
SAKRA-KUMÁRI-KÁ ...	Near Renuká-tirtha about sixteen miles to the north of Nahan in the district of Sirmur in the Panjab. The name of Sakra-Kumáriká was used by way of contradistinction to Kanyá-Kumáriká (*Mahábhárat*).
SALÁTURA ...	The birth-place of Pánini, the celebrated grammarian (Hiuen Tsiang). It has been identified by Cunningham with the village of Lahor, which is four miles to the north-west of Ohind in the Panjab.
SALILARÁJA-TIRTHA ...	The place where the Indus falls into the ocean (*Mahabhárat*).

ANCIENT NAMES.	MODERN NAMES OR SITUATION.
SAMANTA-PANCHAKA ...	Same as *Kurukshetra.*
SAMATATA ...	East Bengal.
SAMÁ ...	The river Lohita or Brahmaputra.
SAMBUKA-ÁSRAMA ...	Ramtek, north of Nagpur in Central India, where Sambuka, a Sudra, performed asceticism, for which reason he was killed by Rámachandra (*Rámáyana*).
SAMET-SEKHARA	The Párasnáth hill in the district of Hazaribagh in the Bengal province, the holiness of which is held in great estimation by the Jainas. Páraswanátha, the twenty-third Tirthankar of the Jainas, died here at the age of one hundred years. It was the scene of *Nirvána* of no less than nineteen of the twenty-four Tirthankars.
SAMUGAR ...	Fateabad, nine miles east of Agra (Bernier), where Aurangzebe defeated Dara.
SANKARÁCHÁRYA	The name of a mountain, at present called Takht-i-Suleiman, near Srinagar in Kasmir, where Asoka's son Kunála founded a monastery, and where the celebrated reformer Sankarácharya established Siva worship.
SANKARA-TIRTHA ...	In Nepal, immediately below the town of Patan at the confluence of the Váchmati and the Manimati : Siva is said to have performed asceticism at this place for obtaining Durgá.

ANCIENT NAMES.	MODERN NAMES OR SITUATION.
SANKHODDHÁRA	The island of Bati, belonging to the province of Guzerát, situated at the south-western extremity of the gulf of Cutch. Vishnu is said to have destroyed a demon named Sankhásura at this place, and to have restored the Vedas (R. K. Roy).
SAPTAGRÁMA ...	Sátgáon: an ancient town of Bengal near Magrá in the district of Hugli: it is now an insignificant village consisting of a few huts. It was a great emporium of commerce at the time of the Romans.
SAPTA-KULA-CHALA	The seven principal mountains, which are Mahendra, Malaya, Sahya, Suktimána, Gandhamádana, Vindhyá and Páripátra.
SAPTA-MOKSHA-DÁPURI ...	The seven holy towns are Ayodhyá, Mathurá, Máyá, Kási, Kánchi, Avanti, and Dwárávati.
SARAJU ...	The Ghágrá or Gográ. The town of Ayodhyá is situated on this river.
SARASWATI	1. The river Saraswati rises in the hills of Sirmur and emerges into the plains at Ad Badri, deemed sacred by the Hindus. It disappears for a time in the sand near the village of Chalaur and re-appears at Bhawanipur. At Balchhappar it again disappears, but re-appears again at Bara Khera; at Urnai, near Pehoa, it is joined by the

ANCIENT NAMES.	MODERN NAMES OR SITUATION.
	Márkanda, and the united river still bearing the name of Saraswati, ultimately joins the Ghaggar (*Punjab Gazetteer*). 2. A river near Somnáth in Guzerát. 3. Arachosia (Rawlinson).
SARÁVATI	1. The river Sabarmati in Guzerát, which falls into the Gulf of Cambay. Ahmedabad stands on this river. 2. Fyzabad in Oudh (Dr. R. L. Mitra's *Lalita-vistara*), but Sarávati appears to be the corruption of Srávasti (modern Sáhet-Máhet) on the Rápti (compare the *Rámáyana* and the (*Raghuvansa*).
SARVANA ...	About twenty miles south-east of Unao in Oudh, where Dasaratha, king of Ayodhyá, killed Rishi Sarvana, or Sindhu, the son of a blind Rishi (*Rámáyana*).
SASASTHALI ..	Antraveda,—the Doab between the Ganges and the Jamuna.
SATADRU ...	1. The river Sutlej: it is also called the Ghaggar or the Ghara. 2. Sirhind in the Pánjab.
SAURÁSHTRA ...	The peninsula of Guzerát, the Surastrene of the Greeks. It comprised the country from Sindh or Indus to Baroach: Guzerát, Cutch and Katiwar.
SAUVIRA ...	It has been identified by Cunningham with Eder, a town in the province of Guzerát which was Vadari of the Buddhist period. Sauvira was the Sophir of the Bible. According to another writer, Sauvira was situated between the Indus and the Jhelum.

ANCIENT NAMES.		MODERN NAMES OR SITUATION.
SÁKADWIPA	...	Central Asia : the country of the Sakas.
SÁKALA	...	The capital of Madra-desa. It has been identified by Cunningham with Sanglawala-Tiba on the Apagá river west of the Rávi in the Panjab.
SÁKAMBHARI	...	1. Mewar. 2. Sambhára in Rajputana, where a well called Deodáni is pointed out as the identical well in which Devayáni, the queen of Rájá Yayáti, was thrown by her co-wife Sarmishthá.
SÁKETA	...	Oudh. Its capital was Sujanakot or Sanchankot, the Sha-chi of Fa Hian, thirty-four miles north-west of Unao in Oudh (Führer).
SÁLAGRÁMA	...	A place situated near the source of the river Gandak, where Bharata and Rishi Pulaha performed asceticism.
SÁLIVÁHANA-PURA	...	Pattana *(see Pratisthána).*
SÁNKALA	...	Same as *Sákala.*
SÁNKÁSYA	...	Sankisa or Sankisa Basantapur, situated on the river Ikshumati, now called the Káli-Nadi, between Atranji and Kánouj, and twenty-three miles west of Fathgarh in the district of Farrakhabad. It was the capital of Rájá Kusadhwaja, brother of Siradhwaja Janaka, the father of Sitá of the Rámáyana. It was a famous place of Buddhist pilgrimage, as it was here that Buddha descended from the Trayastrinsa heaven by the ladder of gold, accompanied by the gods Indra and Brahmá (Cunningham and Führer).

ANCIENT NAMES.	MODERN NAMES OR SITUATION.
SÁNTA-TIRTHA ...	At Gungeswari ghát in Nepál, where the river Maradáriká joins the Váchmati or Bágmati. Párvati is said to have performed penance at this place.
SÁRIKÁ ..	One of the 52 Pithas, where Sati's throat is said to have fallen. The temple of Sáriká Devi is situated on the Hari mountain, three miles from Srinagar in Kásmir. It was the hermitage of Rishi Kásyapa (see *Kásyapapura* .
SEKA ...	The country about Jhajpur, south-east of Ajmir (Yule). But the Mahábhárat places it to the south of the Charmanavati (Chambal) and north of Avanti (Ougein) : it was conquered by Sahadeva, one of the Pándavas.
SETIKÁ ...	Ayodhyá (Oudh). Setiká is evidently a corruption of Sáketa.
SETUBANDHA ...	Adam's Bridge between India and Ceylon, said to have been built by Ráma with the assistance of Sugriva for crossing over to Lanká.
SIARH	Nathadwar on the Banas, twenty-two miles north-east of Udayapur in Mewar, where the ancient image of Kesava Deva was removed from Mathura by Ráná Ráj Singh in anticipation of Aurangzebe's raid (Tod and Growse).
SIDDHAPURA ...	1. Siddhaur, sixteen miles west of Bára Banki in Oudh. 2. Sitpur (Sidpur) in Guzerát, the hermitage of Rishi Karddama and birth-place of Kapila.

ANCIENT NAMES.	MODERN NAMES OR SITUATION.
SIDDHÁSRAMA ...	Buxar in the district of Shahabad. Vishnu is said to have incarnated as Vámana (dwarf) at this place. On the bank of a small stream called Thorá, near its junction with the Ganges, on the western side of Buxar, is a small mound of earth which is worshipped as the birth-place of Vámana Deva (*Rámáyana* and *Brahmánda Purán*). A fair is held here every year in the month of Bhádra in honor of Vámana Deva. A fair is also held in honor of Vámana Deva at Fatwa, situated at the confluence of the Ganges and the Punpun, in the district of Patna, where large numbers of people bathe on a festival called Bárani Dawádasi. 2. The hermitage of Suta on the bank of the Achchhoda-saroavara in Kásmir (see *Achchhoda-sarovara*).
SINDHU ...	1. The river Indus. 2. Sindh. 3. The river Sindh in Malwa called Dakshina Sindhu in the Mahábhárat. The name of India (Intu of Hiuen Tsiang) is a corruption of Sindhu or Sapta Sindhu (the Hafta Hindu of the Arabs).
SINHALA ...	Ceylon. The *Dipavansa* relates the conquest of the island by Vijaya, who came from Lála or Guzerát (in 483 B. C.)
SINHAPURA ...	It has been identified by Cunningham with Katas or Katáksha, which is sixteen miles from Pindi Dadan Khan on the north side of the Salt range in the Panjab. According to Hiuen Tsiang, the country

ANCIENT NAMES.		MODERN NAMES OR SITUATION.
		of Sinhapura bordered on the Indus on its western side : it was a dependency of Kásmir in the seventh century. It was conquered by Arjuna.
SIPRÁ	...	The river on which Ougein stands.
SITADRU	...	The river Sutlej.
SITÁ	...	The river Yarkand or Zarafshan on which the town of Yarkand is situated.
SITÁPRASTHA	...	The river Dhabalá (see *Báhudá*).
SIVISTHÁNA	...	Sawan on the right bank of the Indus.
SOMA-PARVATA		1. The Amarkantaka mountain in which the river Nerbuda has got its source (*Amara-kosha*). 2. The southern part of the Hala range along the Lower Valley of the Indus (*Rámáyana*).
SOMA-TIRTHA	...	Prabhása (see *Prabhása*).
SOMESWARA-GIRI		The mountain in which the river Bángangá has got its source.
SONAPRASTHA	...	Sonepat (see *Kurukshetra*).
SONÁ	...	The river Sone : it was the western boundary of Magadha. It formerly joined the Ganges a little above Bankipur, the western suburb of Patna, from which its embouchure is now sixteen miles distant and higher up the Ganges McCrindle).
SONITAPURA	...	The ancient Sonitapura is still called by that name, and is situated in Gárwal on the bank of the river Kedár-Gangá or

Mandákini, about six miles from Ushámat, and at a short distance from Gupta-Kasi. Ushámat is on the north of Rudra-Prayága, and is on the road from Hardwar to Kedárnáth. A dilapidated fort still exists at Sonitpur on the top of a mountain, and is called the fort of Rájá Vána. Sonitapura was the capital of Vána Rájá, whose daughter Ushá was abducted by Aniruddha, the grandson of Krishna (*Harivansa*). Dr. Führer says that Kotalgarh in the district of Kumaon is pointed out as the stronghold of Vánásura.

A ruined fort situated at Damdamá on the bank of the river Punarbhavá fourteen miles to the south of Dinajpur, is called "Vána Rájá's garh," and it is said to have been the abode of Rájá Vána, whence they say Ushá was abducted by Aniruddha, and various arguments are brought in to prove this assertion. But the route of Krishna from Dwáriká to Sonitapura as given in the *Harivansa*, and the description of the place as being situated on a mountain, do not support the theory that Damdamá was the ancient Sonitapura. An inscription found in the fort proves that it was built by a king of Gour of the Kámboja dynasty. Vána Rájá's fort in the district of Dinajpur is as much a myth as the *Uttara-gogriha* (northern cowshed) of Rájá Viráta at Kántanagar in the same district. The Assamese also claim Tejpur as the ancient Sonitapura.

ANCIENT NAMES.		MODERN NAMES OR SITUATION.
SRÁVASTI	...	Sáhet-Máhet. On the southern bank of the river Rápti (Irávati): it was the capital of Uttara-Kosala, fifty-eight miles north of Ajodhyá *Rámáyana*). It was the Savatthipura of the Buddhists. Buddha resided here for twenty-five years.
SRIKANTHA	...	Same as *Kurujángala*. Its capital was Bilàspur, thirty-three miles north-west of Sáharanpur.
SRIKSHETRA	..	Puri in Orissa. Ananga Bhima Deo of the Gangá dynasty built the temple of Jagannáth in 1198 A. D. He reigned between 1175 and 1202 A. D. The Gangávansi kings reigned in Orissa, after the Kesari kings, from 1132 to 1534 A. D.; the first king of the dynasty was Chorgangá and the last king was a son of Pratápa Rudra Deva, who died in 1532, and who was a contemporary of Chaitanya (Hunter's *Orissa*). The temple of Bimalá at Puri is one of the 52 Pithas, where a fragment of Sati's body is said to have fallen.
SRINAGARA	....	The capital of Kásmir built by Rájá Pravarasena about the beginning of the sixth century of the Christian era.
SRINGAVERA-PURA	....	Singraur on the river Ganges, eighteen miles north-west of Allahabad. It was the residence of Guhaka Nisháda, who was the friend of Dasaratha and Ráma.
SRIRANGA-KSHETRA		Same as *Srirangam*.

ANCIENT NAMES.	MODERN NAMES OR SITUATION.
SRIRANGAM ...	Seringham on the north of Trichinopoly in the province of Madras It contains the celebrated temple of Sri Rangam, an image of Vishnu. The temple was built by the kings of the Nayak dynasty of Pándya.
SRIRANGA-PATTANA ...	Seringapatam in Mysore.
SRI-SAILA ...	The Palni hills in Madura, which form the northern portion of the Malaya mountain.
SRUGHNA ...	Kálsi, in the Jaunsár district, on the east of Sirmur (Beal). Cunningham identifies Srughna with Sugh, near Kálsi, forty miles from Tháneswar, and twenty miles to the north-west of Saharanpur.
STAMBAPURA ...	Támralipta or Tamluk.
STAMBA-TIRTHA	Kambay.
STHÁNESWARA	Thaneswar (see *Kurukshetra*).
STHÁNU-TIRTHA	Same as *Stháneswara*.
SUBHADRÁ ...	The river Iráwadi.
SUBHAVASTU ...	Same as *Suvástu*.
SUCHAKSHU ...	The river Oxus: it was also called Vakshu.
SUDÁMÁPURI ...	Porebandar in Guzerát.
SUDHÁPURA ...	Soonda in North Canara (Thornton).

ANCIENT NAMES.	MODERN NAMES OR SITUATION.
SUKARA-KSHETRA ...	Soron, twenty seven miles north-east of Itah in the Itah district, where Hiranyáksha was slain by Vishnu in his incarnation as Varáha (boar). It contains a temple of Varáha-Lakshmi. Tulsi Dás, the celebrated Hindi poet, was reared up at this place during his infancy when he was deserted by his parents.
SUKTIMÁNA-PARVATA ...	That portion of the Vindhyá range which joins the Páripátra and the Riksha-parvata, including the hills of Bindhyáchal in the district of Mirzapur.
SUKTIMATI ...	1. The river Suvarnarekhá in Orissa. 2. The river Betwá in Malwa, which flows through the ancient kingdom of Chedi (Chanderi).
SULAKSHINI ...	The river Chandrávati or Goga which falls into the Ganges.
SUMANA-KUTA ...	Adam's Peak in Ceylon (Monier Williams).
SUMERU-PARVATA ...	The Rudra-Himalaya where the river Ganges has got its source. It is also called Pancha-Parvata from its five peaks: Rudra-Himalaya, Vishnupuri, Brahmapuri, Udgárikantha, and Swargárohini. Four of the five Pándavas died at the last mountain (see *Gangotri*).
SUMHA ...	Sumha has been identified by some authors with Arracan; but it appears from the sixth chapter of *Dasakumáracharita*

ANCIENT NAMES.	MODERN NAMES OR SITUATION.
	that Dámalipta was the principal town of Sumha, and according to the *Hema-kosha*, Dámalipta was another name of Támralipta or Támalipta (Tamluk). Hence Sumha was the *country* of Támralipta. There was another country by the name of Sumha in the Panjáb conquered by Arjuna.
SUNDHA-DESA ...	Tipárá and Arracan.
SURASENA ...	The kingdom of which Mathura was the capital.
SURÁSHTRA ...	1. Guzerát (see *Saurásthra*). 2. Surat.
SURPÁRAKA ...	It has been identified by Cunningham with Surat. Dr R. L. Mitra identifies Surpárika of the Buddhist period with Sipeler (Sippára of Ptolemy), a seaport near the mouth of the Krishna (*Lalita-vistara*). But the Chaitanya-charitámrita places it to the south of Kolhapur. McCrindle places it (Soupara) about one hundred miles to the south of Surat near Paum in his map of *Ancient India*.
SURYANAGARA	Srinagar in Kásmir. The Mahomedans changed the name into Srinagar (Bernier's *Travels*, Constable's Ed., p. 397, note).
SURYAPURA ...	Surát (*J. A. S. B.*, Vol. VI, p. 387, J. Prinsep).
SUSHOMÁ ...	The river Sindh in the Panjáb.
SUSHUNI ..	The Rajmahal hills in Bengal.

ANCIENT NAMES.	MODERN NAMES OR SITUATION.
SUVARNABHUMI	Burma (Beal). But Fergusson identifies it with Thatun on the Sitang river, forty miles north of Martaban : it was the Golden Chersonese of the classical geographers. The Mahāwanso relates that after the third Buddhist synod in 246 B.C., Asoka despatched two missionaries, Sono and Uttaro, to Subarna-bhumi for proselytising the land.
SUVARNAGRÁMA	Sonárgáon in Vikrampur in the district of Dacca, situated on the opposite side of Munshigunge, on the river Dhaleswari.
SUVÁMÁ ...	The river Rámgangá in Oudh and Rohilkhand.
SUVÁSTU ...	1. The Swat river,—the Suastos of the Greeks. Pushkarávati or Pushkalávati, the capital of Gándhára or Gandharva-desa, stood on this river near its junction with the Kabul river. 2. Swat. Buddhist writers included Swat in the country of Udyána. It was at Swat that Rájá Sibi of the Mahábhárat and the Sivi-játaka gave his own flesh to the hawk to save the dove.
SYANDIKA ..	The river Sai, seven miles south of Jaunpur and twenty-five miles north of Benares (P. N. Ghosal's *Travels*).

T

TAILANGA ...	Same as *Telingana*.
TAKKA-DESA ...	Between the Vipásá and the Sindhu rivers : the Panjáb (Hiuen Tsiang). It was the country of the Báhikas (*Rájá-tarangini*).

ANCIENT NAMES.		MODERN NAMES OR SITUATION.
TAKSHASILA	...	Taxila. General Cunningham places the site of the city near Shah-dheri, one mile north-east of Kála-ká-serai between Attock and Rawalpindi, where he found the ruins of a fortified city. St. Martin places it at Hasan-Abdul, eight miles north-west of Shah-dheri. It is said to have been founded by Taksha, the son of Bharat and nephew of Rámachandra. The Kathá-saritságara places it on the bank of the Vitastá (Jhelum).
TAMASÁ	...	The river Tonse between the Saraju and the Goomti, which, flowing through Azamgarh, falls into the Ganges. The bank of this river is associated with the early life of Válmiki, the author of the *Rámáyana*.
TANUSRI	...	Tenasserim, the southern division of the province of Lower Burma.
TAPANI	...	The river Tápti.
TATINI	...	The Chikakol river in the Circars.
TÁMASAVANA	...	It has been identified by Cunningham with Sultanpur in the Pánjab. Beal places it at the confluence of the Sutlej and the Beas. It was at the Támasavana convent that the fourth Buddhist synod was convened by Kaniksha under the presidency of Vasumitra (Beal's *Introduction to Fa Hian*). The date of this convention (78 A. D.) has given rise to the Saka era.
TÁMRALIPTA	...	Same as *Támralipti*.

ANCIENT NAMES.		MODERN NAMES OR SITUATION.
TÁMRALIPTI	...	1. Tamluk on the river Selai, just above its junction with the river Hugli (Wilson). It formerly bordered on the sea. 2. South Bengal (R. C. Dutt).
TÁMRAPARNI	...	1. Ceylon of the Buddhists. 2. The river Támbraparni in Tinnevelly.
TÁPI	...	The river Tápti.
TELINGANA	...	The country between the Godávari and the Krishna, which is now the territory of the Nizam. McCrindle supposes that Telingana is a contraction of Tri-Kalingana or Tri-Kalinga (see *Andhra*).
TILAPRASTHA	...	Tilpat, six miles to the south-east of Toghlakabad, and ten miles to the south-east of the Kutab Minar. It was included within Indraprastha, the capital of Yudhisthira. Shaikh Faridi Bukhari built Faridábád near Delhi on the greater part of the old parganah of Tilpat (Blochmann's *Ain-i-Akbari*). It was one of the five villages demanded by Yudhishthira from Durjodhana.
TILODAKA	...	Tilárá, a village on the east bank of the Phálgu, visited by Hiuen Tsiang, thirty-three miles to the south-west of Patna.
TIRABHUKTI	...	Tirhut (see *Videha*).
TIRTHAPURI	...	Twenty-one miles from Darchin in the Himalaya, on the bank of the Sutlej. Bhasmásura is said to have been killed at this place: a heap of ashes is pointed

ANCIENT NAMES. MODERN NAMES OR SITUATION.

out as the remains of that Asura (Fraser). The place of Bhasmásura's death is also pointed out in a cave situated in a hill near Sasiram in the district of Shahabad. Bhasmásura obtained a boon from Mahádeva to the effect that whoever he would touch upon the head should at once be consumed to ashes. He wanted to try the efficacy of the boon by touching the head of Mahádeva himself, —the giver of the boon. Mahádeva fled, pursued by Bhasmásura, and took the protection of Vishnu, who advised the Asura to make the experiment by placing his hand upon his own head instead of that of another. He followed the advice, and was at once consumed to ashes.

TRIGARTTA ... Jálandhar, a part of the district of Lahore, according to Wilson; but Wilford identifies the place with Tahora. Tahora or Tihora is situated on the river Sutlej, a few miles from Ludhiana, where excellent ruins were observed by Captain Wade (*J. A. S. B.*, Vol. VI). Kangra is supposed by some to be the ancient Trigartta.

TRI-KALINGA .... Same as *Telingana*.

TRIMALLA ... Tirumala, six miles west of Tirupati or Tripati in the district of North Arcot. The celebrated temple of Bálájí (Lakshmana) is situated on a mountain called Sesáchala. The Pápanásini-Gangá rises in this mountain.

ANCIENT NAMES.		MODERN NAMES OR SITUATION.
TRIPADI	...	Tirupati or Tripati in the province of Madras: it is a place of pilgrimage (*Chaitanya-charitámrita*)
TRIPURI	...	1. Teor on the river Nerbuda. It was the capital of Rájá Kokalladeva, who founded it in the ninth century of the Christian era. 2. Chedi.
TRISROTÁ	...	1. The river Tistá in the district of Rungpur. 2. The river Ganges (*Amarakosha*).
TRITIYÁ	...	The river Tistá.
TULUNGA	...	South Canara.
TULUVA	...	South Canara.
TUNGABHADRA		A branch of the Krishna, on which Kiskindhyá is situated.

U

UDAKHANDA	...	Ohind on the Indus in the Peshawur division of the Panjáb.
UDAYAGIRI	...	A mountain which is five miles from Bhuvaneswara in Orissa. It is a spur of the Assiá range (ancient Chatushpitha) containing many Buddhist sculptures of a very ancient date (*J. A. S. B.*, Vol. XXXIX.)
UDRA	...	Orissa.

ANCIENT NAMES.	MODERN NAMES OR SITUATION.
UDYÁNA ...	Udyána was situated to the north of Peshawur on the Swát river, but it is probable that it covered the whole hill-region south of the Hindu Kush and the Dard country from Chitral to the Indus. Swát. Mangala was the capital of Udyána.
UGRA ...	Kerala.
UJÁLIKANAGARA	Jais, twenty miles east of Rai Bereli.
UJJAINI ...	Ougein, the capital of Avanti, which was the kingdom of Rájá Vikramáditya (515 to 550 A. D.) It is situated on the river Siprá. The celebrated temple of Mahákála (Mahádeo), mentioned by Kálidasa in his Meghaduta, is situated in this town.
UJJÁNAKA ...	Kafristan: a country situated on the river Indus immediately on the west of Kásmir (*Mahábhárat*). Ujjánaka is evidently a corruption of Udyána.
UJJAYANTA ...	Mount Girnár, close to Junágar in Kattiwár. It is sacred to Neminâth, the twenty-second Tirthankara of the Jainas (see *Girinagara*).
UPAMALLAKA ...	Malacca.
URAGAPURA	Negapatam (Nágapattana): it was the capital of Pándya in the sixth century (*Raghuvansa*).
URAGÁ	Same as *Urasá*.
URASÁ ...	In the Hazára country between the Bidaspes (Jhelum) and the Indus (*Mahábhárat*).

ANCIENT NAMES.		MODERN NAMES OR SITUATION.
URANJIRÁ	...	The Vipásá (Beas).
URAVILWA	...	Buddha-Gayá, six miles to the south of Gayá. It was here that Buddha attained Buddhahood, below the celebrated Pipal tree *(Ficus religiosa)*, called also the Bodhi tree, immediately on the west of the temple, which was built between the fifth and the seventh centuries of the Christian era. Fergusson supposes that the temple was built by Amara Deva (the author of the *Amara-kosha*), who was one of the "nine gems" in the court of Vikramáditya who reigned in Malwa from 515 to 550 A. D. (*History of Indian and Eastern Architecture*, p. 69). The Muchilinda tank, now called Buddha-kunda, is situated to the south of the temple; and the place where Buddha walked up and down after attaining Buddhahood, is marked by a plastered parapet, now called Jagamohan, situated almost immediately on the north side of the temple. The temple faces east, and is one of the most graceful temples in India. Sákyá attained Buddhahood at the age of thirty-six in 522 B. C.
UTKALA	...	Orissa.
UTPALÁRANYA		Bithoor, fourteen miles from Cawnpur, where the hermitage of Válmiki was situated. It was at this place that Sitá, the wife of Rámachandra, gave birth to Lava and Kusa. It is the site of the celebrated city called Pratishthána, which was ruled by Rájá Uttánapada, the father of

ANCIENT NAMES.	MODERN NAMES OR SITUATION.
	Dhruva. The remains of a fort here, on the bank of the Ganges, are pointed out as the fort of Rájá Uttánapada.
UTPALÁVATA-KÁNANA ...	Same as *Utpalâranya* (*Márkandeya Purán*).
UTPALÁVATI ...	The river Vypar in Tinnevelly.
UTTARAGÁ ...	The river Rámagangá in Oudh (N C. Dás.)
UTTARA-KURU	The northern portion of Gurwal and Hundesa.
UTTÁNIKA ...	The Rámagangá in Oudh (N. C. Dás).

V

VADARI ...	The O-cha-li of Hiuen Tsiang. It has been identified by Cunningham with Eder in the province of Guzerát: it was Sauvira of the Paurânic period.
VAIRÁTA-PATTANA ...	The capital of the old kingdom of Govisana, visited by Hiuen Tsiang in the seventh century. It has been identified with Dhikuli in the district of Kumaon (Führer's *Monumental Antiquities and Inscriptions*, p. 49).
VAISALI	Besarh in the district of Mozaffarpur (Tirhut), eighteen miles north of Hájipur, on the left bank of the Gandak. The parganá Besárá, which is evidently a

ANCIENT NAMES. MODERN NAMES OR SITUATION.

corruption of Visálá, is situated within the sub-division of Hájipur. Vaisali was the name of the country as well as of the capital of the Vrijjis (Vájjis) or Lichhavis who flourished at the time of Buddha. Buddha lived in the Mahávana monastery, which was situated near the present village of Bakhra, about two miles north of Besarh, and near it was the tower called Kutágár (double storeyed) built over half the body of Ánanda. About a mile to the south of Besarh was the mango-garden which was presented to Buddha by the courtesan Ámradáriká, called also Ambapáli Chapala was about a mile to the north-west of Besarh, where Buddha hinted to Ánanda that he could live in the world as long as Ánanda liked, but the latter did not ask him to live (Bigandet's *Life of Gaudama*).

VAKSHU ... The river Oxus.

VANAVÁSI ... Mysore was called by this name during the Buddhist period.

VANÁYU ... Arabia (T. N. Tarkaváchaspati)

VARÁHA-KSHETRA ... 1. Barámula in Kásmir, where Vishnu is said to have incarnated as Varáha (the boar). There is a temple of Mahádeo Koteswara (see *Sukara-kshetra*). 2. Another place of the same name exists in the district of Purnea, below the Triveni (see *Mahá-Kausika*).

ANCIENT NAMES.		MODERN NAMES OR SITUATION.
VARENDRA	...	Rájshahi in Bengal.
VARSÁNA	...	Barsán in the district of Mathura, where Rádhiká, the favourite milk-maid of Krishna, was born.
VASISHTHA-ÁSRAMA	...	The hermitage of Rishi Vasishtha was situated at Mount Abu (see *Arbuda*), and also at a place one mile to the north of the Ajodhya station of the Oudh and Rohilkhand Railway.
VATSYA	...	A country situated to the west of Allahabad. It was the kingdom of Rájá Udayana: its capital was Kausámbi.
VATSYA-PATTANA	...	Kausámbi, the capital of Vatsya-desa—the kingdom of Vatsya Rájá and Udayana (*Kathá-saritságara*).
VÁCHMATI	...	The river Bágmati in Nepal. Eight Tirthas out of the fourteen great Tirthas of Nepál have been formed by the junction of the Bágmati with other rivers. The names of the eight Tirthas are: Panya, Sánta, Sankara, Raja, Chintámani, Pramadá, Satalakshana, and Jayá. The source and exit of the Bágmati are two other Tirthas. Same as *Bhágavati*.
VÁHIKA	...	A country between the Beas and the Sutlej, north of Kekaya. It is another name of Válhika (see *Takka-desa*)
VÁLHIKA	...	1. A country between the Beas and the Sutlej, north of Kekaya. Váhika is the corrupted form of this name. 2. Balkh,—the Bactriana of the Greeks.

ANCIENT NAMES.	MODERN NAMES OR SITUATION.
VÁLMIKI-ÁSRAMA ...	Bithoor, which was the hermitage of Rishi Válmiki, the author of the Rámáyana. Sitá, the wife of Rámachandra, lived at the hermitage during her exile, where she gave birth to the twin sons, Lava and Kusa. The temple erected in honor of Válmiki at the hermitage is situated on the bank of the Ganges. Sitá is said to have been landed by Lakshmana while conveying her to the hermitage at the Sati-ghát in Cawnpur. A large metallic arrow-head of a greenish colour is shown in a neighbouring temple at Bithoor, also situated on the bank of the Ganges, as the identical arrow with which Lava wounded his father, Rámachandra, in a fight for the *aswa-medha* horse: this arrow-head is said to have been discovered a few years ago in the bed of the river Ganges.
VÁRANÁVATA ...	Barnáwá, nineteen miles north-west of Mirát, where an attempt was made by Duryodhana to burn the Pándavas (Führer).
VÁRÁNASI ...	Benares. In the seventh century it was visited by the celebrated Chinese traveller Hiuen Tsiang. He has thus described the city and its presiding god Bisweswara: "In the capital there are twenty Deva temples, the towers and halls of which are of sculptured stone and carved wood. The foliage of trees combine to shade (the sites), whilst pure streams of water encircle them. The

ANCIENT NAMES. MODERN NAMES OR SITUATION.

statue of Deva Maheswara, made of *teou-shih* (brass), is somewhat less than 100 feet high. Its appearance is grave and majestic, and appears as though really living." The present Bisweswara, which is a mere *linga*, dates its existence since the original image of the god, described by Hiuen Tsiang, was destroyed by that iconoclast Aurangzebe and thrown into the Gyánbápi, a well situated behind the present temple.

VÁRÁNASI-KATAKA ... Cuttack in Orissa, at the confluence of the Mahánadi and the Kátjuri, founded by Nripa Kesari, who reigned between 941 to 953 A. D. The former capitals of the Kesari kings were Bhuvaneswara and Jájpur (Hunter's *Orissa*.

VÁSISHTHI ... The river Gumti.

VEDAGARBHA-PURI ... Buxar in the district of Shahabad in the province of Bengal (*Brahmánda Purán* and *Skanda Purán*). The word Buxar, however, seems to be the contraction of Byághrasara, a tank attached to the temple of Gouri-sankara, situated in the middle of the town.

VEDAVATI .. The river Dámudá in Bengal.

VENGI ... The capital of Andhra, situated north-west of the Elur lake, between the Godávari and Krishna rivers. It is now called Vegi.

VENI .. The Krishna : same as *Venwá*.

ANCIENT NAMES.	MODERN NAMES OR SITUATION.
VENUVANA-VIHARA ...	The monastery was built by king Bimbisára in a bamboo grove situated on the north-eastern side of Rajgir and presented to Buddha, where he resided when he visited the town after attaining Buddhahood.
VENWÁ ..	1. The Bena, a branch of the Krishna, which rises in the Western Ghats. 2. The Krishna. 3. The river Waingangá, a tributary of the Godávari, which rises in the Vindhyapáda range (*Márkandeya Purán*).
VESSANAGARA ...	Besnagar, close to Sanchi in the kingdom of Bhopal. It is also called Chetyagiri in the Mahawanso. Asoka married Devi, the daughter of the chieftain of this place, while on his way to Ujjaini, of which place, while a prince, he was nominated governor. By Devi, he had twin sons, Ujjenio and Mahindo, and a daughter Sanghamitta. The two last named were sent by their father to introduce Buddhism into Ceylon with a branch of the Bodhi-tree of Buddha-Gayá. Asoka was the grandson of Chandragupta of Pátaliputra, and he reigned from 276 to 240 B. C. (Turnour's *Mahawanso* and Fergusson's *History of Indian and Eastern Architecture*).
VETRAVATI ...	The river Betwa in Malwa.
VIDARBHA ..	1. Berar, the kingdom of Bhishmaka, whose daughter Rukmini was married to Krishna. Its principal towns were

ANCIENT NAMES.	MODERN NAMES OR SITUATION.
	Kundinanagara and Bhojakatapura. 2. Beder.
VIDARBHA-NAGARA ...	Same as *Kundinapura*.
VIDEHA ...	Tirhoot, the kingdom of Rájá Janaka, whose daughter Sitá was married by Rámachandra. Its other name was Mithilá. Mithilá was the name both of the country and the capital. Janakpur was the capital of Rájá Janaka. About a mile to the north of Sitámárhi, there is a tank which is pointed out as the place where the new born Sitá was found by Janaka while he was ploughing the land. Panaura, three miles south-west of Sitámárhi, also claims the honor of being the birth-place of Sitá. About six miles from Janakpur is a place called Dhenuká, now overgrown with jungles, where Rámachandra is said to have broken the bow of Hara. Videha was bounded on the east by the river Kausiki (Kusi), west by the river Gandaka, north by the Himalaya, and south by the Ganges.
VIDISÁ ...	Bhilsa in Malwa in the kingdom of Bhopal on the river Betwa (Vetravati). The Bhilsa topes, including the topes at Sanchi, belong to a period ranging from 250 B. C. to 79 A. D.
VIDYÁNAGARA ...	1. Bijayanagar on the river Tungabhadra, formerly the metropolis of the Brahminical kingdom of Bijayanagar or Karnáta. It was founded by Buka and Aka Harihar in 1336. 2. Vijayanagara

ANCIENT NAMES.	MODERN NAMES OR SITUATION.
	(see *Padmávati*) at the confluence of the Sindhu and the Pára in Malwa. 3. Rájamahendri on the Godávari (*Journal of the Buddhist Text Society*, Vol. V).
VINÁ ...	1. The river Krishna, the Tynna of the Greeks. 2. Almorah in Kumaon.
VINDHYA-PÁDA	The Satpura range (*Váyu Purán*).
VINDHYÁCHALA	The Vindhya range. The celebrated temple of Vindubásini is situated on a part of the hills near Mirzapur: it is one of the stations of the E. I. Railway. The temple of Yogamáyá, which is one of the 52 Pithas, where the toe of Sati's left foot is said to have fallen, is at a short distance from the temple of Vindubásini. Yogamáyá, after she warned Kansa, king of Mathura, of the birth of Krishna, came back to the hills and took her abode at the site of the temple of Vindubásini. The town of Vindhyáchala was included within the circuit of the ancient city of Pampápura (Führer).
VIPÁSÁ ...	The Beas,—the Hyphasis of the Greeks. The origin of the name of this river is related in the Mahábhárat: Rishi Vasishtha, being weary of life on account of the death of his sons, who were killed by Viswámitra, tied his hands and feet with cords, and threw himself into the river, which, afraid of killing a Bráhmana, *burst his bond*, and brought him to the shore.

ANCIENT NAMES. MODERN NAMES OR SITUATION.

VIRASARA Bilsar, about twenty-two miles to the north of Sánkásya, where Buddha passed the twelfth *wasso* (*varshá*) or rainy-season retirement).

VIRÁTA ... Bairát, one hundred and five miles to the south-west of Delhi, and forty-one miles to the north of Jeypur (Cunningham). It was the capital of Viráta Rájá, king of Matsyadesa, where the five Pándavas lived in secrecy for one year. It is a mistake to identify Viráta with Dinájpur, where at Kántanagar Viráta's *Uttara-gogriha* (northern cowshed) is shown, the *dakshina-gogriha* (southern cowshed) being shown at Midnapur, as such identification is not countenanced by the Mahábhárat, which relates that Yudhishthira selected a kingdom in the neighbourhood of Hastinápura as his place of concealment, from which he could watch the movements of his enemy Duryodhana. See *Matsyadesa*.

VITASTÁ ... The river Jhelum,—the Hydaspes of the Greeks.

VISÁKHÁ ... Oudh was called by this name during the Buddhist period.

VISÁLA-CHHATRA ... Same as *Visálá*. Hájipur was included in the kingdom of Visálá. Rámachandra, Lakshmana and Viswámitra, on their way to Mithilá, are said to have halted at Hájipur on the site of the present temple, which contains the image of

ANCIENT NAMES. MODERN NAMES OR SITUATION.

Rámachandra on the western side of the town. Háji Ilayas Shamsuddin, king of Bengal, established his capital at Hájipur in the middle of the fourteenth century, and from him the name of Hájipur is derived. The celebrated Rájá Toran Mal made it his residence when he made the settlement of Bengal and Behar. Sonpur, situated at the confluence of the Gandak and the Ganges, was also included in Visála-chhatra. It was at Sonpur that Vishnu is said to have released the elephant from the clutches of the alligator, the fight between whom has been described in the Mahábhárat. Rámachandra, on his way to Janakapura, is said to have raised a temple on the spot, and dedicated it to Mahádeo Harihara Náth, in honor of whom the celebrated fair is held every year (Hunter's *Stat. Acct. of Bengal*, Vol. XI, p. 262).

VISALÁ ... Besarh, in the district of Mozaffarpur, the Vaisali of the Buddhist period (see *Vaisali*).

VISWÁMITRA-ÁSRAMA ... Buxar in the district of Shahabad in Behar. It was the hermitage of Rishi Viswámitra, where Rámachandra is said to have killed the Rákshasi Táraká. The Charitra-vana at Buxar is said to have been the hermitage of the Rishi, and the western side of Buxar near the river Thorá was the ancient Siddhásrama, the reputed birthplace of Vámana Deva

ANCIENT NAMES.	MODERN NAMES OR SITUATION.
	(see *Siddhásrama*). The hermitage of Rishi Viswámitra is also pointed out at Devakunda, twenty-five miles north-west of Gayá.
VRAJA ...	Gokul, the water-side suburb of Mahábana—a village in the neighbourhood of Mathura across the Jamuna, where Krishna was reared by Nanda during his infancy. The name of Vraja was extended to Vrindávana and the neighbouring villages, the scene of Krishna's early life and love. The shrine of Syám Lálá is believed to mark the spot where Jasodá, the wife of Nanda, gave birth to Máyá or Joga-nidrá, substituted by Basudeva for the infant Krishna. Outside the town is Puatná-khar, where Krishna is said to have killed Putaná. Growse identifies Mahábana with Klisoboras of the Greeks and supposes that the modern Vraja was the ancient Anupa-desa. Varsána was the birth-place of Rádhiká, the favourite Gopi of Krishna.
VRINDÁVANA ...	Brindaban in the district of Mathura, the scene of Krishna's love with the Gopis. The original image of Govindaji was removed to Jeypur and that of Madanmohan to Karauli in anticipation of the raid of Aurangzebe. The old temple of Govindaji was built by Mán Singh in the thirty-fourth year of Akbar's reign (Growse).
VYÁSA-ÁSRAMA...	Manal, a village near Badrináth in the Himalaya. It was the hermitage of Rishi

ANCIENT NAMES.	MODERN NAMES OR SITUATION.
	Vyása, the author of the Mahábhárat, and the reputed author of the Puráns
VYÁSA-KÁSI ...	Rámnagar, opposite to Benares across the Ganges. The temple dedicated to Váysa Rishi is situtated within the precincts of the palace of the Mahárájá of Benares

---

Y

YAMUNOTRI ...	A spot in the Bándara-puchchha (monkey's tail) mountain in the Himalaya, where the river Jamuna has its source. It has reference solely to the sacred spot where the worship to the goddess Jamuna is performed. The Jamuna rises from several hot springs, and the spot for bathing is at the point where the cold and warm waters mingle and form a pool (see *Kalinda-desa*).
YASAPURA ...	Same as *Yessavul.*
YASHTIVANA ...	Jethian, about two miles north of Topoban in the district of Gaya (Grierson). It is also called Jaktiban (Cunningham). Buddha is said to have displayed many miracles at this place.
YAVA-DWIPA ..	The island of Java. It is said to have been colonised by a prince of Guzerát.
YAYÁTIPURI ...	Jajmaw, three miles from Cawnpur, where the ruins of a fort are pointed out as the remains of the fort of Rájá Yayáti (see *Sákambhari*). The temple of Siddhináth Mahádeo is at a short distance from the fort.

ANCIENT NAMES.	MODERN NAMES OR SITUATION.
YÁJNAPURA ...	Jajpur in Orissa on the river Baitarani. It is said to have been founded by Rájá Yayáti Kesari in the sixth century. Jajpur is a contraction of Yayátipura (pronounced Jajátipura). It was the capital of the Kesari kings till the tenth century, when the seat of government was removed to Cuttak by Nripa Kesari. The temple of Birajá at Jajpur is one of the 52 Pithas where a part of Sati's body is said to have fallen.
YESSAVUL ...	Ahmedabad was founded on the site of the ancient city of Yessavul by Ahmed Shah of Guzerát in 1412 (Thornton's *Gazetteer*). Yessavul is evidently a corruption of Yasapura (pronounced Jasapura). Ahmedabad was also anciently called Karnávati (Fergusson).

II.

MODERN NAMES

OF

ANCIENT INDIAN GEOGRAPHY,

BEING AN

APPENDIX

TO

The Geographical Dictionary of Ancient and Mediæval India.

BY

NUNDO LAL DEY,

Of the Bengal Judicial Service.

Calcutta:
PRINTED AND PUBLISHED BY W. NEWMAN & CO.,
AT THE CAXTON STEAM PRINTING WORKS, 1, MISSION ROW.

[illegible].

PREFACE.

For the plan of this work, I have been indebted to the suggestion of Mr. J. D. Cargill, C. S., Sub-Divisional Officer of Buxar, now District Magistrate of Noakhali. The present work will afford facility for finding out the ancient places from their modern names. I have taken this opportunity to make considerable additions both in the names and in the accounts of places, and to supply many omissions which occurred in my Geographical Dictionary of Ancient and Mediæval India: hence the present work may not be inappropriately called an Appendix to the Geographical Dictionary. The subject is so vast that it is not likely that full justice can be done to it by a single individual, and notwithstanding one's attempt to make much of the materials at hand, a work like this must necessarily remain incomplete. Many of the places mentioned in ancient Hindu and Buddhist works have not yet been identified, and most of them defy identification. My attempt in the Geographical Dictionary as well as in the present work, feeble as it may be, has been to make a systematic arrangement and collection of facts regarding ancient places which have been identified, in order to make them useful to the public as works of easy reference.

CHATRA.
27th August, 1899.

NUNDO LAL DEY.

MODERN NAMES

OF

ANCIENT INDIAN GEOGRAPHY.

AN APPENDIX

TO

The Geographical Dictionary of Ancient and Mediæval India.

MODERN NAMES.	ANCIENT NAMES OR SITUATION.
	A.
ABU ...	Arbuda-parvata, a detached mount of the Aravali range, in the Sirohi state of Rajputana. It was the hermitage of Rishi Vasishtha. It is also one of the five hills sacred to the Jainas as containing the temples of Rishabhanath or Adinath, the first Tirthankara and Neminath, the twenty-second Tirthankara.
ACHCHHAVAT ...	Achchhoda-sarovara in Kásmir, six miles from Marttanda, described by Bánabhatta in his Kádamvari. Marttanda is situated about five miles to the east of Islamabad, the ancient capital of Kásmir. The Siddhásrama was situated on the bank of this lake.
ADAM'S BRIDGE ...	Setubandha between India and Ceylon, said to have been constructed by Rámachándra with the assistance of Sugriva for crossing over to Lanká.

MODERN NAMES.	ANCIENT NAMES OR SITUATION.
ADAM'S PEAK ...	1. Rohana, 2. Sumana-kuta in Ceylon.
AFGHANISTAN ...	1. Kámboja, 2. Kaofu (Kambu) of Hiuen Tsiang, 3. Loha of the Mahábhárat, 4. Rohi.
AGASTIPURI ..	Agastya-ásrama,—the hermitage of Rishi Agastya, twenty-four miles to the south-east of Nasik.
AGRA ...	Agravana, one of the eighty-four Vanas of Vraja.
AHIÁRI ...	1. Gautama-ásrama, 2. Ahalyásthána, in pargana Jarail, twenty-four miles to the south-west of Janakpur in Tirhut. It was the hermitage of Rishi Gautama, where Indra ravished his wife Ahalyá.
AHMEDABAD ...	1. Yasapura (Jasapura), 2. Yessavul, 3. Karnávati in Guzerát on the river Sabarmati (ancient Sarávati).
AHMEDNAGAR ...	Bingar, seventy-one miles from Poona.
AIRWA ..	1. Álavi of the Buddhists, 2. Álabhi of the Jainas, twenty-seven miles north-east of Itawa in the North-Western Provinces, where Buddha passed his sixteenth *wasso* (*varshá* or rainy-season retirement). Mahávira, the last Tirthankara of the Jainas, made his missionary peregrinations from this place. It is the A-lo of Fa Hian.
AJAYA ...	The river Ajamati in Bengal.

MODERN NAMES.		ANCIENT NAMES OR SITUATION.
AJMIR	...	Ajamera (*Bhavishya Purán*).
AJUNTA	...	Achinta, about fifty-five miles to the north-east of Ellora in Central India. In the Achinta monastery resided Árya Sanga, the founder of the Yogáchárya school of the Buddhists (S. C. Das's *Indian Pandits in the Land of Snow*) It is celebrated for its caves and vihárs, which belong to the fifth and sixth centuries of the Christian era.
ALIGARH	...	Koel.
ALLAHABAD	...	1. Prayága, 2. Bharadwája-ásrama, the hermitage of Rishi Bharadwája. The celebrated Akshaya-Bata (the undecaying banian tree) was visited by Hiuen Tsiang in the seventh century.
ALOPI	...	The temple of Alopi is situated at Allahabad: it is one of the 52 Pithas. It is the ancient Prajápati-vedi of the Mahábhárat, a celebrated place of pilgrimage.
ALWAR	..	1. Matsya-desa, 2. Machheri, which is a corruption of Matsya, the kingdom of Rájá Viráta of the Mahábhárat, in whose court Yudhishthira and his brothers resided *incognito* for one year. The Alwar state formerly appertained to the territory of Jeypur. There is still a town called Machheri in this state. The capital of Matsya-desa was Viráta, now called Bairat, forty-one miles to the north of Jeypur and one hundred and five miles to the south-west of Delhi.

MODERN NAMES.	ANCIENT NAMES OR SITUATION.
AMARAKANTAKA	Bansagulma at the source of the river Nerbuda in the Amarakantaka mountain. The sacred *Kunda* of Bansagulma is situated four miles and a half to the east of the source of the Nerbuda.
AMARAKANTAKA MOUNTAIN ...	1. The Mekala mountain, 2. the Soma mountain, in which the river Nerbuda has its source.
AMARANÁTH ...	The celebrated temple of Amarnátha is situated in a natural grotto of the Haramuk mountain of the Bhairavagháti range of the Himalaya at Gungabal in Kasmir. The grotto is said to be full of wonderful congelations, where blocks of ice, stalagmites, formed by the dripping water from the roof, are worshipped as images of Siva.
AMARÁVATI ...	1. Dhanakataka, 2. Dhamnakataka, 3. Dhányakataka, 4. Dhányavatipura, 5. Dharmakota, 6. Dhanakakota have been identified with Dharanikota, one mile to the east of Amarávati in Central India. It was the capital of Andhra. The Buddhist saint Bhávaviveka resided here awaiting the advent of Maitreya Buddha.
AMER ...	Ambara, the ancient capital of Jeypur, which was called Dhoondra. The capital was removed to Jeypur in 1728 A. D. by Siwai Jey Singh.
AMI ...	One of the 52 Pithas, eleven miles to the east of Chhapra.

MODERN NAMES.	ANCIENT NAMES OR SITUATION.
AMIN ...	1. Abhimanyu-khera, 2. Chakrabyuha of the Mahábhárat, where Abhimanyu, son of Arjuna, was killed at the celebrated battle of Kurukshetra. It was included in Kurukshetra.
ANAGANDI ...	Konkanapura, the capital of Konkana or Kankana, on the northern bank of the Tungabhadra river (Cunningham).
ANURÁDHÁPURA	The ancient capital of Ceylon. The branch of the celebrated Bo-tree (Pipar-tree) of Buddha-Gayá was brought and planted here by Mahindo and his sister Sanghamitta, who were sent by their father Asoka to introduce Buddhism into Ceylon in the reign of the king Devánámpiyatissa (Turnour's *Mahawanso*). The tree still exists in the Mahá Vihára. The left canine tooth of Buddha, which was removed from Dantapura (Puri) in the fourth century to Anurádhápura, still exists in a building erected on one of the angles of Thuparamaye Dagoba (*Dhátugarbha*) which was built by Devánámpiyatissa about 250 B. C. as a relic-shrine of the right jaw-bone of Buddha (Fergusson). The town contains also the Lowa Maha Paya or Great Brazen Monastery described in the Mahawanso; it was built by the king Duttagaimuni in the second century of the Christian era.
ARABIA ...	Vanáyu.

MODERN NAMES.		ANCIENT NAMES OR SITUATION.
ARAVALI	...	Arbuda-parvata in Rajputana: its branches terminate at the north at Delhi. A part of the range was called Devagiri. The Aravali range was included in Páripátra or Párijátra.
ARRAH	...	Árámanagara in the district of Shahabad in Bengal.
ASHTÁBAKRA-NADI	...	The river Samangá, a small river which flows by the side of Raila, ten miles from Hardwar.
ASSAM	...	Kámarupa: its capital was Pragjyotishapura.
ASSIA RANGE	...	Chatush-pitha Parvata in Orissa. Udayagiri is a spur of this range, five miles from Bhuvaneswara, containing many Buddhist sculptures of a very ancient date (*J. A. S. B.*, Vol. XXXIX).
AUMI	...	It has been identified by Cunningham with the river Anomá (Anamala) in the district of Gorakhpur, which was crossed by Buddha, after he left his father's palace, at a place now called Chandaoli on the eastern bank of the river, whence Chhandaka returned with Buddha's horse Kantaka to Kapilavastu.
AURANGABAD	...	1. Janastháua of the Rámáyana, 2. Kharki of the Mahomedan historians.
AURANGABAD-HILLS	...	Prasravanagiri, situated on the bank of the Godavari, graphically described by

MODERN NAMES.		ANCIENT NAMES OR SITUATION.
		Bhavabhuti in the Uttara-Rámacharita. In one of the peaks of the hills dwelt Jatáyu of the Rámáyana.
AYUK-NADI	...	The Apagá river to the west of the Rávi in the Panjab.

B.

BÁBLÁ	...	The river Bakreswari which falls into the Ganges near Katwa in Bengal.
BADRINÁTH	...	Badarikásrama on the bank of the Bishengangá (Alakánandá) in Gurwal. It was the hermitage of Vyása, the author of the Mahábhárat. It contains the celebrated temple of Nara-Náráyana.
BÁGESWAR	...	In the district of Kumanu in Oudh, near the junction of the Ganges and the Gomati. It was the hermitage of Márkanda Rishi.
BÁGMATI	...	1. The river Váchmati, 2. the Bhágmati, 3. the Bhágavati, 4. the Kakouttha of the Buddhists in Nepal.
BÁGPAT	...	Bhágaprastha, thirty miles to the west of Mirat, one of the five villages demanded by Yudhishthira from Duryodhana.
BAIBHÁRA-GIRI	...	Vaihára-giri, one of the five hills of Rajgir in Bihar: Webháro of the Buddhists.
BAIDYANÁTH	...	I. Chitábhumi in Bengal: it is one of the 52 Pithas. II. Kárttikeyapura in the district of Kumaon.

MODERN NAMES.	ANCIENT NAMES OR SITUATION.
BAKRAUR ...	Gandha-hasti stupa, on the Phalgu, opposite to Buddha-Gayá. It was visited by Hiuen Tsiang.
BALARAMAPUR ...	Ramgarh-Gaura, twenty-eight miles north-east of Gonda in Oudh.
BALIA ...	1. Bhrigu-ásrama, 2. Bagrásana, the hermitage of Rishi Bhrigu in the district of Balia in the North-Western Provinces. 3. It was a part of Dharmáranya. At a short distance to the north-east corner of Balia, there is a tank called Dharmáranya-Pokhrá, and to the north and east of it there are traces of an ancient jangal or scrubby forest. At Balia there is a temple dedicated to Bhrigu Rishi, containing the impressions of his feet.
BALKH ...	1. Váhlika, 2. Bactriana of the Greeks.
BALLABHI ...	1. Balabhi, 2 Dhank, 3. Mongy-pattana, the ancient capital of Sauráshtra or Guzerát, ten miles north-west of Bháonagar. It was destroyed in the sixth century at the time of Siláditya (Tod). Bhatti, the celebrated author of the Bhatti-kávya, flourished in the court of Sridharasena I, king of Balabhi in the fifth century. Bhattrihari is also said to have been the author of the Bhatti-kávya. The Ballabhi dynasty from Bhatárka Senápati (a general of Skanda Gupta of Kanouj) to Siláditya IV reigned from 465 to 718 A. D. (Fergusson).

MODERN NAMES.		ANCIENT NAMES OR SITUATION.
BALTISTAN	...	Bolor: same as *Little Thibet.*
BAMILAPUR	...	Same as *Ballabhi.*
BANAS	...	The river Parnásá in Rajputana.
BÁNDAR-PUCHCHHA	...	The mountain called Bándar-puchchha on the Himalaya, in which the river Jamuna has its source, is situated in the country which was called Kalinda-desa: hence the Jamuna is called Kálindi.
BÁRA-BANKI	...	Jasnaul in Oudh, from Jas, a Rájá of the Bhar tribe, who is said to have founded it in the tenth century.
BARAGÁON	...	Nálanda, seven miles north of Rájgir, in the district of Patna. Nágárjuna, the celebrated author of the *Mádhyamika Sutras* containing the tenets of the Maháyána school of Buddhism and editor of the original *Susruta*, resided in the Nálanda monastery in the first or second century of the Christian era, making it the principal seat of Buddhist learning for Central India.
BARÁMULA	....	.1 Varáhamula, 2. Varáhakshetra, in Kásmir on the Jhelum, thirty-two miles to the north-west of Srinagar, where Vishnu is said to have incarnated as the boar. 3. Hushkapura, founded by Hushka or Huvishka, the brother of Kaniksha. There is still a village called Uskara, which is two miles to the south-east of Barámula (Cunningham).

MODERN NAMES.	ANCIENT NAMES OR SITUATION.
BÁRI-DOAB ...	Between the Rávi and the Sutlej. It comprised the ancient country of Parvata.
BARNAGAR ...	1. Bara-pura, 2. Ánandapura of Hiuen Tsiang, one hundred and seventeen miles to the north-west of Balabhi in Guzerát (St. Martin).
BARNÁWA ...	Váranávata, nineteen miles north-west of Mirat, where an attempt was made by Duryodhana to burn the Pándavas.
BAROACH ...	1. Bhrigu-kshetra, 2. Bhrigu-ásrama, 3. Bhrigu-kachchha, 4. Bharu-kachchha, 5. Barygaza of the Greeks: it was the hermitage of Bhrigu Rishi.
BARSÁN ...	Varsána in the district of Mathura was the birth-place of Rádhiká, the favourite Gopi of Krishna.
BASUDHÁRÁ ...	The source of the Alakánandá, about four miles to the north of Badrináth, near the village Mánál.
BAY OF BENGAL	Mahodadhi (*Raghuvansa* and *Váyu Purán*).
BEAS ...	1. The river Vipásá, 2. the Arjikeya, 3. the Uranjirá, 4. the Hyphasis of the Greeks, in the Panjab.
BELLARI ...	Balahari, south of the river Tunga-bhadra.
BENARES ...	1. Váránasi, 2. Kási. Kási was originally the name of the country, and Váránasi was its capital.

MODERN NAMES.	ANCIENT NAMES OR SITUATION.
BENGAL ...	1. Banga, 2. Gour, from its capital of the same name near Máldá. Ancient Banga was divided into five provinces: Pundra or North Bengal, Samatata or East Bengal, Karna-suvarna or West Bengal, Támralipta or South Bengal, and Kámarupa or Assam (R. C. Dutt). That part of Bengal which lies to the west of the Ganges was called Rára. The Pála Rájás from Bhupála to Sthirapála reigned in Bengal from the middle of the ninth to the twelfth century of the Christian era, and the Sena Rájás from Ádisura or Vira Sena to Lakshmaniyá or Surasena reigned from 994 to 1203 A. D. The poet Jayadeva, the author of the *Gita Govinda*, and the lexicographer Haláyudha flourished in the court of Lakshmana Sena in the twelfth century.
BERAR ...	1. Bidarbha of the Purans, 2. Dakshina Kosala of the Buddhist period (Cunningham). Its capitals were Kundina-nagara and Bhojakatapura.
BESARH ...	1. Visálá, 2. Visálá-chhatra of the Purans, 3. Vaisali of the Buddhist period, in the district of Muzaffarpur (Tirhut) in the province of Bengal, eighteen miles north of Hajipur on the left bank of the Gandak. Vaisali was the name of the country, as well as of the capital of the Vrijjis (Vájjis) or Lichhavis, who flourished at the time of Buddha who resided here for some time.

MODERN NAMES.	ANCIENT NAMES OR SITUATION.
BESNAGAR ...	Chetyagiri or Wessanagara (Vessanagara) of the *Mahawanso*, close to Sanchi in the kingdom of Bhopal, where Asoka married Devi and by her he had twin sons, Ujjenio and Mahindo, and afterwards a daughter, Sanghamitta.
BETWA ...	The river Vetravati in Malwa.
BEYT ISLAND ...	1. The island of Sankhoddhára. 2. Bati, situated at the south-western extremity of the gulf of Cutch. Vishnu is said to have destroyed a demon named Sankhásura at this place. Sankhásura was the husband of Tulsi, who was transformed into the Basil plant by the curse of Vishnu, and Vishnu was transformed into the Sálagráma stone by her curse.
BHÁGALPUR ..	1. The country about Bhágalpur in the province of Bengal, was called Anga, 2. Karnapura.
BHAIGU ...	The river Kapivati of the Rámáyana, a tributary of the Ramaganga in Oudh.
BHILSA ...	Vidisá in Malwa. The Bhilsa topes are supposed by Fergusson to belong to a period ranging from 250 B. C. to 79 A. D.
BHIMÁ ...	The river Bhimrathi, a branch of the Krishná. It was also called Bhimarathá.
BHOJAPUR ...	I. The name was indiscriminately applied to both the capitals of ancient Vidarbha, namely, Kundinapura and Bhojakatapura (compare the *Harivansa*

MODERN NAMES.	ANCIENT NAMES OR SITUATION.
	and the *Raghuvansa*). II. Near Dumraon in the district of Shahabad in the Province of Bengal. Wilson identifies it with the ancient Márttikábat, but the place has got no tradition beyond the Mahomedan period: the *Nava-ratna*, evidently a Mahomedan structure, is the only ancient building at this place.
BHOOTAN ...	Bhotanga.
BHUVANESWAR	1. Ekámrakánana, 2. Harakshetra, in Orissa: it was founded by Rájá Yayáti Kesari in the latter part of the fifth century.
BIHAR ...	1. Magadha, 2. Kikata. Its ancient capital was Girivraja or Rájagriha (Rajgir) at the time of the Mahábhárat, but the seat of government was removed to Pataliputra by Udayáswa, grandson of Ajátasatru.
BIJAYANAGAR ...	I. 1. Padmávati, 2. Padmapura, 3. Vidyánagara at the confluence of the Sindh and Parbati in Malwa. It was the birth-place of the poet Bhavabhuti. The scene of the *Málati-mádhava* has been placed at Padmávati. II. Hampi on the river Tungabhadra (see *Vijayanagara*).
BIJNOR ...	Kanwa-ásrama: the hermitage of Rishi Kanwa, who adopted the celebrated Sakuntalá as his daughter.
BIKANER ...	Bágar-desa in the Pánjab (Cunningham).

MODERN NAMES.	ANCIENT NAMES OR SITUATION.
BILASPUR ...	Thirty-three miles north of Saharanpur. The district of Bilaspur was 1. Kurujángala of the Mahábhárat, 2. Srikantha of the Buddhist period.
BILSAR ...	Virasara of the Buddhists, about twenty-two miles to the north of Sánkásya, where Buddha passed the twelfth *Wasso.*
BINDU-SARA ...	A sacred pool two miles south of Gangotri in the Rudra-Himalaya, where Bhagiratha is said to have performed asceticism to bring down the goddess Gangá from heaven.
BITHA ...	Bitabhayapattana, eleven miles south-west of Allahabad. It was an ancient Buddhist town.
BITHOOR ...	1. Válmiki-ásrama, 2. Pratishthána, 3. Utpaláranya, 4. Utpalábata-kánana, fourteen miles north-west of Cawnpur on the river Ganges. It was the capital of Rájá Uttánapáda, father of the celebrated Dhruva, and the hermitage of Válmiki, the author of the Rámáyana, where Sitá, wife of Ràmachandra, gave birth to Lava and Kusa.
BLACK PAGODA	Same as *Kanarak.*
BODH-GAYA ...	1. Uravilwa, 2. Buddha-Gayá, six miles to the south of Gaya, where Buddha attained Buddhahood below the celebrated Pipal tree called the Bodhi-tree to the west of the temple. The *Vajrásana*, on which Buddha is said to

MODERN NAMES.	ANCIENT NAMES OR SITUATION.
	have sat while he gave himself up to contemplation, is a stone seat situated between the Bodhi-tree and the temple. The Buddhakunda to the south of the temple is the ancient Muchilinda tank. The rail to the south of the temple is one of the most ancient sculptured monuments in India.
BRAHMA-GIRI ...	That part of the Western Ghats in which the river Godávari has its source.
BRAHMAJONI ...	1. The Brahmayoni hill, 2. the Koláhala-parvata, 3. the Koláchala, 4. the Gayasirsa at Gaya was the Buddhist Gayasisa mountain where Buddha delivered his "burning" sermon, or, as it is called, the Sermon of the Mount. On the site of Asoka's stupa on the top of the hill, the Hindus have now built a temple of Chandi.
BRAHMAKUNDA	The Kúnda from which the river Brahmaputra issues: it is a place of pilgrimage.
BRAHMAPUTRA	1. The river Hladini, 2. the Lohitya, 3. the Samá.
BRINDABAN ...	In the district of Mathura, the scene of Krishna's love with the Gopis.
BUDDHAKUNDA.	The Muchilinda tank in Buddha-Gayá to the south of the temple, on the western bank of which Buddha sat for seven days in contemplation after attaining Buddhahood.

MODERN NAMES.	ANCIENT NAMES OR SITUATION.
BUDHAIN ...	Buddhavana, about six miles north of Tapoban in the district of Gaya.
BURHA-RAPTI ...	1. The river Báhuda, 2. the Dhabalá, 3. the Sitáprastha, 4. the Arjuni,—a feeder of the Rápti in Oudh. Same as *Dhumelá*.
BURMAH ...	1. Suvarnabhumi, 2. Brahma-desa.
BUXAR ...	1. Vedagarbhapuri, 2. Siddhásrama, the hermitage or birth-place of Bámana Deva, one of the incarnations of Vishnu, near the junction of the Thorá and the Ganges; 3. Viswámitra-àsrama, the hermitage of Viswámitra, where Táraká was killed by Rámachandra; 4. Vyághra-sara, from a tank near the temple of Gourisankara in the town. Buxar is situated in the district of Shahabad on the line of the East India Railway.

C

CABUL VALLEY	The country of the lower Cabul valley, lying along the Cabul river between the Khoaspes (Kunar) and the Indus, formed what was called the Gandharva-desa of the Rámáyana, and the Gándhára of the Mahábhárat and the Buddhist period. It comprised the districts of Peshawur and Hoti-Mardan, as the district of Mardan is called, known as the Eusufzoi country. Its ancient capital was Pushkalávati (modern Hashtanagar, eighteen miles north of Peshawur), and its second

MODERN NAMES.		ANCIENT NAMES OR SITUATION.
		capital was Purushapura (modern Peshawur). Near the junction of the Indus and the Cabul rivers was the ancient Gonardda-desa, in which Salátura (modern village Lahor), the birth-place of the celebrated grammarian Pánini, is situated.
CACHAR	...	Hiramba.
CAGGAR	...	The river Drishadvati, mentioned in Manu and the Puráns as the southern boundary of Kurukshetra, now absorbed in the sands between Jessalmer and Rori Bakher.
CALCUTTA	...	The name of Calcutta is derived from Káli-ghát, one of the 52 Pithas.
CANARA	...	South Canara was called (1) Tulunga, (2) Tuluva.
CANDAHAR	...	The "New Gándhára," where the begging pot of Buddha was removed from Kaniksha's dagoba at Peshawur—the "true Gándhára"—and is still said to be preserved there by the Mussalmans (Rawlinson).
CARNATIC	...	The part of the Carnatic which lies between Ramnad and Seringapatam was called Karnáta.
CENTRAL ASIA		Sáka-dwipa, the country of the Sakas.
CEYLON	...	1. Singhala, 2. Lanká, 3. Ratnadwipa, 4. Támraparni, 5. Serendwipa.

MODERN NAMES.	ANCIENT NAMES OR SITUATION.
CHAKARNAGAR	Ekachakrá of the Mahábhárat, sixteen miles south-west of Itawa in the N.-W. Provinces.
CHAKRA-TIRTHA	I. In Kurukshetra. II. In Prabhása in Guzerát. III. Six miles from Tryambaka, which is near the source of the Godavari.
CHAMBAL ...	The river Charmanavati in Rájputana. The Chambal has its source in a very elevated point of the Vindhya amongst a cluster of hills which are called Janapava. It has three co-equal sources from the same cluster, the Chambal, Chambela and Gambhira (Tod). The river is said to have been formed by the blood of the cows sacrificed at the *Yajna* of Ranti Deva.
CHAMPÁNAGAR	1. Champápuri, 2. Champá, 3. Málini, 4. Champá-Malini, near Bhagalpur in Bengal: it was the capital of Anga, the kingdom of Lomapáda of the Rámáyana and Karna of the Mahábhárat. It is also associated with the story of Behulá and Nakhindar.
CHANDERI ...	1. Chedi, 2. Tripuri, the capital of Sisupála of the Mahábhárat, in Malwa.
CHANDRAGIRI ...	Near Belligola, not far from Seringapatam, sacred to the Jainas.
CHAUSA ...	Chyabana-ásrama in the district of Shahabad in Bengal: it was the hermitage of Rishi Chyabana (*Váyu Purán*).

MODERN NAMES.		ANCIENT NAMES OR SITUATION.
CHAYENPUR	...	Chandapura, five miles to the west of Bhabua in the district of Shahabad in Bengal. It was the residence of Chanda and Munda of the *Chandi*.
CHENAB	...	1. The river Asikni, 2. the Acesines of the Greeks, 3. the Chandrabhágá, 4 the Chandriká, in the Panjab.
CHHATISGARH	...	1. Dasárna, 2. Desarena Regio of the Periplus.
CHHOTA-GANDAKA	...	1. The river Ajitavati, 2. the Hiranyavati, on the north of Kusinagara where Buddha died.
CHHOTA-NAGPUR	...	1. Mundá (*Váyu Purán*), 2. Jhárakhanda (*Chaitanya-charitámrita*), 3. Kokrah of the Mahomedan historians. The Mundás of the present day reside particularly in the district of Ranchi in the Chhota (Chutia) Nagpur division.
CHIDAMBARA	...	In South-Arcot, the birth-place of Sankaráchárya according to the *Sankara-Digvijaya*.
CHIKAKOL	...	Srikakola in the Northern Circars.
CHITRAL	...	Bolor.
CHITTAGONG	...	1. Chattala, 2. Phullagráma.
CHITTELDURG		Chitra-durga.
CHOYA	...	The river Kárttiki, a branch of the Saraswati, mentioned in the Mahábhárat.

MODERN NAMES.		ANCIENT NAMES OR SITUATION.
CHUKA	...	The river Málini in Oudh (Griffiths).
CHUNAR	...	1. Charanádri, 2. Chandelgara in the district of Mirzapur (N.-W. P.) The fort of Chunar was built by the Pála Rájás of Bengal. The portion of the fort called Bhattrihari's palace is said to have been originally the hermitage of Bhattrihari, the disciple of Vasuráta and author of the *Bairágya Sataka*.
CIRCARS	...	Included in the ancient Kalinga. The southern portion of the Circars was called Mohana-desa.
COLGONG	...	Durvásá-ásrama: the hermitage of Rishi Durvásá was situated on a hill at the distance of a mile from Colgong in the district of Bhagalpur in Bengal.
COMILLA	...	Kamalinga in Tipárá.
COMORIN	...	1. Kumári, 2. Kumáriká, 3. Kanyá-Kumáriká in contradistinction to Sakra-Kumáriká in the Himalaya.
CONJEVERAM	...	1. Kánchipura, 2. Kánchi, in the province of Madras: it was the capital of Chola or Drávida which extended from Madras to Seringapatam and Cape Comorin. Sankaráchárya died at this place.
COROMANDEL	...	1. Chola, 2. Dravida, between the rivers Kaveri and Krishna: its capital was Kánchipura. Coromandel is the corruption of Cholamandala.
CRANGANORE	...	Kurangalura, a town in Malabar.

MODERN NAMES.		ANCIENT NAMES OR SITUATION.
CURUGODE	...	Kuntala-desa in the province of Madras.
CUTCH	...	1. Audumvara, 2. Kachchha: its ancient capital was Koteswara, or Kachchheswara.

D

DABHOI	...	Darbhavati in Guzerát.
DALKISOR	...	1. The river Dwárikeswari, 2. the Dwárakesi, a branch of the Rupnarain, near Bishnupur in Bengal.
DÁMUDÁ	...	1. The river Dámodara, 2. Dharmodaya in Bengal.
DARDISTAN	...	Darada, a country between Chitral and the Indus.
DARJILING	...	Durjayalinga: a temple of Mahadeo called Durjayalinga is situated at this place.
DATIHÁ	..	Adhirája of the Mahábhárat in the Gwalior territory It was the kingdom of Dantavakra, who was killed by Krishna. The name of Datihá also indicates the place where Dantavakra was killed. The country was conquered by Sahadeva, one of the five Pándavas. A Vaishnava work places it near Brindaban in the district of Mathura.
DAULI	..	The Dudh-Gangá, a branch of the Alakánandá.

MODERN NAMES.	ANCIENT NAMES OR SITUATION.
DECCAN ...	Dakshinátya: that part of India which lies to the south of the Vindhyá range, the portion between the Himálaya and the Vindhyá being called Aryávartta It was the Dandakavana of the Rámáyana, and Dakshina-patha of Bhavabhuti.
DELHI ...	Old Delhi was 1. Indraprastha, 2. Khándavaprastha, the capital of Yudhishthira: it is still called Indrapat, 3. Jogipura of Chánd Bardai. The *Puráná killá*, or the old fort, is still pointed out as the fort of the Pándavas. It includes a portion of the parganá Tilpat (ancient Tilaprastha), one of the five villages demanded by Yudhishthira from Duryodhana.
DEOGAR ...	Same as *Baidyanath*, in Bengal.
DEVA-PRAYÁGA	At the confluence of the Bhágirathi and the Alakánandá: it is one of the five (*Pancha*) Prayágas.
DEVI-PÁTAN ...	Forty-six miles north-east of Gonda in Oudh. It is one of the 52 Pithas where Sati's right arm is said to have fallen.
DHANK ...	Mangipattana in Guzerát. Same as *Ballabhi*.
DHÁR ...	Dháránagara in Malwa, the capital of Rájá Bhoja, who was a great patron of Sanskrit literature. In his court flourished Kálidása, the author of the *Nalodaya*, Jayadeva, the author of the drama *Prasanna Rághava*, and others (*Bhojapravandha.)*

MODERN NAMES.	ANCIENT NAMES OR SITUATION.
DHARAMPUR ...	Dharmapura, north-east of Damaun and north of Nasik.
DHARANIKOTA...	See *Amarávati*
DHARÁWAT ...	In the district of Gaya, subdivision Jáhánabád, where the Gunamati monastery was situated on the Kunwa hill, visited by Hiuen Tsiang.
DHARMÁRANYA	I. 1. Dharmaprishtha, 2. Dharmmáranya of the Buddhist records, visited by numerous pilgrims, four miles from Buddha-Gayá. II. Portions of the districts of Ghazipur, Balia and Jaunpur were known by the name of Dharmmáranya.
DHIKULI ...	Vairátapattana, the capital of Govisana, in the district of Kumaon.
DHOPAP ...	Dhutapápapura on the Gumti, eighteen miles south-east of Sultanpur in Oudh, where Rámachandra is said to have been cleansed of his sin for killing Rávana, who was a Bráhman, by bathing in the river there. Rámachandra is also said to have expiated his sin of slaying Rávana at Hattia Haran (*Hatyá-harana*) near Kalyanmat, twenty-eight miles south-east of Hardoi in Oudh, where he bathed on his return from Lanká. The Kashtahárini Ghát at Monghir also claims the honor of having cleansed the sin of Rámachandra (*Kurma Purán*).
DHOSI ...	Chyabana-ásrama, six miles south of Narnol in the territory of Jeypur, where

MODERN NAMES.	ANCIENT NAMES OR SITUATION.
	the eyes of the Rishi Chyabana were pierced by Sukanyá, a princess of Anupadesa, whom he afterwards married.
DHUMELÁ ...	1. The river Dhabalá, 2. the Báhudá, 3. the Arjuni, 4. the Sitáprastha,—a feeder of the river Rapti in Oudh. Same as *Burha-Rapti*.
DIBHAI ...	Darbhavati, twenty-six miles south-west of Bulandsahar.
DILDARNAGAR ...	Akhandhá, twelve miles south of Ghazipur.
DIU ...	Devabandara in Guzerát.
DOAB (GANGETIC)	1. Antraveda, 2. Sasasthali between the Ganges and the Jamuna.
DOARHATTA ...	Same as *Kampil*.
DOWLATABAD ...	1. Devagiri, 2. Devagara, 3. Dharagara, 4. Tagara of the Greeks, in Hyderabad. It was founded by Singhana in the eleventh century. Vopa Deva, the celebrated grammarian, and Hemádri flourished in the court of Singhana II, who ascended the throne in 1247 A. D.
DUBAUR ...	Durvásá-ásramá: the hermitage of Durvásá Rishi was situated on a hill, seven miles south-east of Rajauli in the subdivision of Nowada, district Gaya.

MODERN NAMES.	ANCIENT NAMES OR SITUATION.
DWARKA ...	1. Dwáriká, 2. Dwárávati, 3. Kusasthali in Guzerát It was the capital of Krishna; he founded it after his flight from Mathura when attacked by Jarásandha, king of Magadha: hence he is worshipped there as Ranchhora-náth. 4. Tod has also identified Dwarka with Kusávati, but this identification is doubtful, as Kusávati was situated on the border of the Vindhyá hills.

E.

EASTERN GHATS	1. Mályavána-giri, 2. Mahendra-parvata. Its southern portion was called Dardara.
EDAR ...	1. Sauvira of the Mahábhárat, 2. Sophir of the Bible, 3. Vadari of the Buddhists, in Malwa.
EKALINGA ...	Hárita-ásrama, the hermitage of Rishi Hárita, the author of one of the Sanhitás. It is situated in a defile about six miles north of Udaipur in Rajputana.
ELLICHPUR ...	1. Bhojakatapura, 2. Bhojapura,—the second capital of Vidarbha.
ELLORA ...	The abode of Ilbala, a demon, who and his brother Vátápi were killed by Agastya. It is situated near Dowlatabad in Central India. The Viswakarmá cave (chaitya) at Ellora and the viháras attached to it are supposed by Fergusson

MODERN NAMES.	ANCIENT NAMES OR SITUATION.
	to belong to a period between 600 to 750 A D., when the last trace of Buddhism disappeared from Western India.

F.

FATEABAD ...	Samugarh, on the Jamuna, nine miles east of Agra, where Aurangzebe defeated Dara.
FEROZABAD ...	1. Chandwar, 2. Chandrapura near Agra, where in 1193 Shahabuddin Ghori defeated Jayachandra, king of Kanouj.

G.

GAHMAR ...	Geha-Mura, in the district of Ghazipur (E. I. Railway): it was the abode of Mura, a demon, who was killed by Krishna.
GÁLAVA-ÁSRAMA	The hermitage of Rishi Gálava was situated at a distance of three miles from Jeypur in Rajputána.
GAMBHIRÁ ...	A branch of the river Chambal near Fatehabad in Malwa, mentioned by Kálidása in his *Meghaduta* (see *Chambal*).
GANDAK ..	1. The river Gandaki, 2. the Sálagrámi 3. the Náráyani.
GANGÁ-SÁGARA	The Ságara-Sangama at the mouth of the Ganges where Kapila destroyed the sons of Sagara by his curse.

MODERN NAMES.		ANCIENT NAMES OR SITUATION.
GANGES	..	The river Gangá
GANGESWARI-GHAT	...	Sánta-tirtha in Nepal at the confluence of the rivers Maradáriká and Bágmati. Párvati is said to have performed penance at this place.
GANGOTRI	..	The source of the river Ganges in the Rudra-Himalaya in Gurwal.
GANJAM	...	Ganjam appertained to the ancient Kalinga, the capitals of which were Manipur (Mánikapattana), Ganjam and Rajamahendri at different periods.
GAYÁ		1. Gayasirsha. 2. The southern portion of the modern town of Gayá was the ancient Gayá. The present temple of Vishnupada was built by Ahalyábái, Mahárání of Indor (1766 to 1795), on the site of an old Buddhist temple: the impression of Vishnu's foot which is worshipped at present was an engraving of Buddha's foot formerly worshipped by the Buddhists. The Brahmajoni hill on the southern side of the town was the Gayasisa or Gayasirsha mountain of the Buddhists, where Buddha delivered his "flaming" sermon to his new disciples after his return from Benares. On the site of Asoka's stupa on the top of the mountain the Hindus have built a temple of Chandi. All the temples in Gayá, containing impressions of feet, where the oblation ceremony is

MODERN NAMES.	ANCIENT NAMES OR SITUATION.
	performed now-a-days, as at Rámsilá hill and other places, were ancient Buddhist temples appropriated by the Hindus after the decay of Buddhism in India. The Surya-kunda near the Vishnupada temple was an ancient Buddhist tank. Brahma-sara of the Mahábhárat is one mile to the south-west from the Vishnupada temple (*Gayá Máhátma*).
GENDIA ...	Gokarna, a town in North Canara, thirty miles to the south of Goa.
GHÁGAR ...	Same as *Sutlej*.
GHÁGRÁ ...	The river Saraju in Oudh: the town of Ajodhya is situated on this river.
GHARA ...	Same as *Sutlej*.
GHAZIPUR ...	The districts of Ghazipur, Jaunpur and Balia in the Norh-Western Provinces appertained to the ancient Dharmáranya (see *Balia*).
GHILGHIT ...	Gahalata.
GIRIYAK ...	Same as *Giryek*.
GIRNÁR ...	1. Raivata, 2. Raivataka, 3. Ujjayanta, 4. Girinagara,—the Junagar hill in Guzerát. It was the hermitage of Rishi Dattátreya. Suta was killed by Balaráma at this place. It is also one of the five hills sacred to the Jainas, containing the temples of Neminách and Páraswanáth.

MODERN NAMES.	ANCIENT NAMES OR SITUATION.
GIRYEK ...	The Indrasilá hill on the southern border of the district of Patna, ten miles to the south of Bihar (town), containing an ancient Buddhist village on the river Panchána. On this hill Indra is said to have questioned Buddha on forty-two points. On one of the peaks of this hill is situated what is called Jarásandha-ka-Baithak, which is a Dagoba or tope (stupa), erected according to Hiuen Tsiang in honor of a Hansa (goose), who sacrificed himself to relieve the wants of a starving community of Buddhist Bhikshus of the Hinayána school. It is Fa Hian's "Hill of the Isolated Rock" (Cunningham).
GOA ...	1. Gova-ráshtra, 2. Gopakavana, which are perhaps the contractions of the ancient Govardhana or Govardhanapura of the Puráns, sacred to Parasuráma.
GODÁVARI ...	1. The river Dakhsina-Gangá, 2. the Gautami, 3. the Gomati. It has its source in the Brahmagiri mountain near the village called Tryambaka.
GODNÁ ...	Gautama-ásrama at Revelganj near Chháprá (see *Akidri*).
GOGA ...	1. The river Chandrávati, 2. the Sulakshini, which falls into the Ganges.
GOGRA ...	Same as *Ghágrá*

MODERN NAMES.	ANCIENT NAMES OR SITUATION.
GOKUL ...	Vraja, four miles south-east of Mathura across the Jamuna where Krishna was reared by Nanda during his infancy. The name of Vraja was extended to Brindában and the neighbouring villages, the scene of Krishna's early life and love. Gokul is the water-side suburb of Mahábana which has been identified by Growse with Klisoboras of the Greeks.
GOLKANDA ...	Gowál-kunda, about seven miles from Hyderabad in the Nizam's territory (Tod). The seat of government was removed from Golkanda to Hyderabad in 1589.
GOMUKHI ...	Fifteen miles north of Gangotri.
GONDA ...	Goura in Oudh : it was a subdivision of Uttara Kosala, the capital of which was Srávasti. The whole of Uttara Kosala was called Goura. The famous tooth-brush (*dantadhávana*) tree of Buddha still exists at Gonda.
GONDWANA ...	Dakshina Kosala (see *Berar*) : it included Wairágarh in the district of Chanda, about eighty miles from Nágpur (Ball).
GONDWANA HILLS ...	The hills of Gondwana were included in the ancient Riksha-parvata.

MODERN NAMES.	ANCIENT NAMES OR SITUATION.
GOUR ...	The ancient capital of Bengal, the ruins of which lie near Máldá at a distance of ten miles. It was also called Lakshmanavati or Laknauti. Gour was also called Rámakeli in the fifteenth century.
GOURI-KUNDA ...	At the confluence of the Kedar-Gangá and the Bhágirathi, at a short distance from Gangotri.
GOWHATI ...	1. Prágjotishapura, the capital of Kámarupa, 2. Kámarupa, 3. Kámakshyá in Assam. It is one of the 52 Pithas.
GREAT DESERT	Marusthali, east of Sindh.
GUMTI ...	1. The river Gomati, 2. the Vásishthi in Oudh.
GUPTÁRA ...	Gopratára on the bank of the Saraju at Fyzabad in Oudh, where Rámachandra is said to have died.
GUZERÁT ...	1. Gurjjara, 2. Sauráshtra, 3. Suráshtra, 4. Ánartta, 5. Láta, 6. Lára or Lála. In the seventh century, when Hiuen Tsiang visited India, the southern parts of Rajputana and Malwa were known by the name of Gurjjara, the modern peninsula of Guzerat being then known by the name of Sauráshtra. The Sah kings of Sauráshtra from Nahapana to Swami Rudra Sah reigned from 79 to 292 A. D. According to Fergusson the

MODERN NAMES.	ANCIENT NAMES OR SITUATION.
	Saka era dates from the coronation of Nahapana, who was a foreigner (*History of Indian and Eastern Architecture*, p. 150). But the convention of the last Buddhist synod by Kaniksha, who was a Saka, was a more remarkable incident of the time than the coronation of such an insignificant king as Nahapana, as it concerned the religion of the whole of India.

H.

HÁJIPUR ...	The sub-division of Hajipur, in the district of Mozaffarpur in the province of Bengal, was called 1. Visálá, 2. Visálachhatra. Rámachandra and Lakshmana are said to have halted at Hajipur on their way to Mithilá at the site of the present temple, which contains the image of Rámachandra, on the western side of the town. Vaisali (Besarh), eighteen miles north of Hajipur, was the capital of the Vrijjis or Lichhavis at the time of Buddha. Sonepur, in the sub-division, was the place where Vishnu released the elephant from the clutches of the crocodile, and on the spot where the fight took place, Rámachandra is said to have raised the temple of Hariharanáth Mahádeo.
HALA MOUNTAIN	The southern part of the Hala mountain along the lower valley of the Indus was called Somagiri.

MODERN NAMES.	ANCIENT NAMES OR SITUATION.
HARDWAR ...	1. Gangádwára, 2. Haradwára, 3. Kanakhala, 4. Máyápuri, 5. Mayura, 6. Haridwára. Though Kanakhala and Máyápuri are at present two different towns and distinct from Hardwar, yet at different periods Hardwára was known by these two names (see *Skanda Purán* and *Meghaduta* of Kálidása). Kanakhala is two miles to the south-east of Hardwar. It was the scene of the celebrated Dakshayajna of the Puráns. Máyápuri is between Hardwar and Kanakhal: it was one of the seven sacred towns of India. The temple of Máyá Devi is situated in Máyápur.
HARI-PARVAT ...	Sáriká, three miles from Srinagar in Kásmir, where the temple of Sáriká Devi, one of the 52 Pithas, is situated. It was the hermitage of Rishi Kásyapa, from whom the name of Kásyapapura or Kásmir was derived.
HASHTÁNAGAR...	1. Pushkalávati, 2. Pushkarávati, 3. Peukelaotes of the Greeks, the old capital of Gándhára or Gandharva-desa, founded by Pushkara, son of Bharata and nephew of Rámachandra. It is situated fifteen miles north-eastward beyond the Kábul river.
HASSAN-ABDUL...	1. Takshasila, 2. Taxila of the Greeks, eight miles north-west of Shahdheri in the Panjab, between Attok and Rawalpindi. The Kathá-saritságara places it

MODERN NAMES.	ANCIENT NAMES OR SITUATION.
	on the bank of the Jhelum. It was founded by Taksha, son of Bharata and nephew of Rámachandra.
HASTINAPUR ...	The capital of the Kurus and of Duryodhana of the Mahábhárat, twenty-two miles north-east of Mirat. Nichakshu, the grandson of Janmejaya, removed his capital to Kausámbi after the diluviation of Hastinápura by the Ganges.
HATTIA HARAN	Hatyá-harana, twenty-eight miles south-east of Hardoi in Oudh (see *Dhopap*).
HAZARA ...	1. Abhisári of the Mahábhárat, 2. Abhisárá, 3. Abisares of the Greeks. The ancient Uraga or Urasa appertained to the country of Hazara.
HAZARIBAGH ...	The eastern portion of the district of Hazaribagh in the province of Bengal appertained to the ancient country of Malladesa.
HIMALAYA ...	1. Himádri, 2. Himáchala.
HINDU-KUSH ...	Nisadha-parvata,—the Paropomisos of the Greeks.
HINGLÁJ ...	Hingulá, situated at the extremity of the Hingulá range on the coast of Mekran in Baluchistan. It is one of the 52 Pithas. Tod says it is nine days' journey from Tatha by Karachi Bunder and about nine miles from the sea-shore.

MODERN NAMES.		ANCIENT NAMES OR SITUATION.
HULLABID	...	Dwára-samudra in Mysore, where the seat of government was removed in the middle of the twelfth century.
HUNDES	...	Same as *Undes*.
HYDERABAD	...	I. Bhágnagara in the Nizam's territory, from Bhágmati, the favourite mistress of Kutab Shah Mahomed Kuli who founded it in 1589, removing his seat of government from Golkonda, about seven miles distant. II. Hyderabad in Sindh has been identified by Cunningham with Patala.

I.

INDIA ...	...	1. Bháratavarsha, 2. Jambudwipa. India (Intu of Hiuen Tsiang) is a corruption of Indu or Sindhu or Sapta Sindhu (*Hapta Hindu* of the Arabs).
INDUS	...	1. The river Sindhu, 2. the Sushomá in the Panjab.
IRAWADI	...	1. The river Irávati, 2. the Pávani, 3. the Subhadrá, in Burma.

J.

JABBALPUR	...	Jávalipattana.
JAIS	...	Ujálikanagara, twenty miles east of Rai Bareli.

MODERN NAMES.	ANCIENT NAMES OR SITUATION.
JÁJMAW ...	Yayátipuri, three miles from Cawnpur, where the ruins of a fort are pointed out as the remains of the fort of Rájá Yayáti (see *Sambhára lake*).
JÁJPUR ...	The country which stretches for ten miles around Jájpur in Orissa was called 1. Birajá-kshetra, 2. Párvati-kshetra, 3. Gayánábhi, 4. Yajnapura, 5. Jajátipura (Yayátipura).
JAKHTIBAN ...	Same as *Jethian*.
JALALABAD ...	Nagarahara, at the confluence of the Surkhar or Surkhrud and Kábul rivers. It is also called Amarávati in one of the Játakas. A village called Nagaraka still exists about two miles to the west of Jalalabad.
JALANDHAR ...	1. Jálandhara, 2. Trigartta in the Pánjab.
JALANDHAR-DOAB ...	Between the Beas and the Sutlej in the Pánjab. It comprised the ancient countries Kekaya, Váhika or Válhika.
JALLALPUR ...	Bukephala of the Greeks in the Pánjab.
JAMUNA ...	1. The river Yamuná, 2. the Kálindi from the country called Kalinda-desa in which it has its source.
JAMUNOTRI ...	The source of the river Jamuna in the Bándarpuchchha range of the Himalaya, situated in the ancient country called Kalinda-desa.

MODERN NAMES.	ANCIENT NAMES OR SITUATION.
JARÁSANDHA-KÁ-BAITHAK ...	Hansa-stupa (see *Giryek*).
JAVA ...	Yava-dwipa.
JETHIAN ...	Yashtivana, about two miles north of Tapoban in the district of Gayá.
JEYPUR ...	The country around Jeypur, including Alwar, was the ancient Matsya-desa of the Mahábhárat. Its capital was Virtáta (modern Bairát) where the Pándavas resided *incognito* for one year: it is a small village to the west of Alwar and forty-one miles north of Jeypur and one hundred and five miles south-west of Delhi.
JHALRAPATTAN	Chandrávati in Malwa on the Chandrabhágá river.
JHELUM ...	1. The river Vitastá, 2. the Behat, 3. the Hydaspes, 4. the Bidaspes of the Greeks, in the Pánjab. It leaves the valley of Kásmir at Barahmula and falls into the Chenab near Jhung.
JHUSI ...	Pratishthánapura, on the north bank of the Ganges, three miles east of Allahabad: it was the capital of Puraravá. It is still called Pratishthápura.
JOGINI-BHARIYA MOUND ...	Jetavana-vihára, one mile to the south of Sáhet-máhet on the Rapti in Oudh, where Buddha resided for several years.
JOHARGANJ ...	Dhanapura, twenty-four miles from Ghazipur.

f

MODERN NAMES.	ANCIENT NAMES OR SITUATION.
JOONIR ...	Jirnanagara in the province of Bombay. The Chaitya cave of Joonir is supposed by Fergusson to belong to the first or second century of the Christian era.
JUNÁGAR ...	1. Javananagara (Yavananagara), 2. Asildurga in Guzerat.
JWÁLÁMUKHI ...	A celebrated place of pilgrimage near Kangra, being one of the 52 Pithas, where Sati's tongue is said to have fallen.
JYNTEA ...	1. Pravijaya, 2. Prágvijaya in Assam.

K.

KÁBUL ...	1. Kubhá of the Vedas, 2. Ortospana of the Greeks, 3. Urddhasthána (Cunningham).
KÁBUL VALLEY	See *Cabul valley*.
KAFRISTAN ...	Ujjánaka: a country situated on the river Indus, immediately to the west of Kásmir.
KAILAS ...	The mountain is situated on the north of Lake Mánas-sarovara beyond Gangri or Darchin. It is also called the Kiunlun range.
KAIMUR HILL ...	The range was called Kimmritya, between the rivers Sone and Tonse.

MODERN NAMES.		ANCIENT NAMES OR SITUATION.
KAJERI	...	1. Kubjagriha, 2. Kajughira, 3. Kajinghara, ninety-two miles from Champa in the district of Bhagalpur.
KÁLÁDI	...	In Kerala, the birth-place of Sankaráchárya, according to the Sankara-vijaya.
KALHUÁ	...	The Makula mountain of the Burmese annals of Buddhism, where Buddha passed his sixth year of Buddhahood. The Kaluhá hill is situated in the district of Hazaribágh, twenty-six miles to the south of Buddha-Gayá and sixteen miles to the north of Chatra. The place abounds with the remains of ancient Buddhist architectures and figures of Buddha. It also contains two impressions of Buddha's feet on the top of the highest peak on the northern side of the valley called *Ákásalochana* and a temple dedicated to Buddha containing his broken image. There are inscriptions also, but they have become obliterated and illegible. On the top of a hill on the western side there is a temple of Durgá called Kuleswari. All the images to be found in the place are the images of Buddha, except that of the goddess Kuleswari. Even the image which is called Bhaironáth is an image of Páraswanáth. There can be no doubt that the Brahmins appropriated this sacred place of the Buddhists and set up an image of Durgá at a subsequent period.

MODERN NAMES.		ANCIENT NAMES OR SITUATION.
KALIANI	...	Kalyána in the province of Bombay It was the capital of the Chalukya kings (western branch) from Jaya Sinha Vijayáditya to Tribhuvana Malla from the fifth to the twelfth century. It was the birth-place of Vijnáneswara, the author of the Mitákshará.
KÁLI-NADI	...	1. The river Ikshumati, 2. the Káli-gangá, 3. the Mandákini in Rohilkhand. Kanouj stands on this river.
KALINJAR	...	1. Kálanjara, 2. Purnadarva, in Bundelkhand. It was the capital of Chedi under the Gupta kings. It contains the temple of Nilakantha Mahádeo.
KÁLI-SCIND	...	The river Pátalávati, a branch of the Chambal in Malwa. It is called Palaitah by Tod. Its identification with Nirvindhyá (*J. B T. S.*, Vol. V., Pt. III., p. 46), which rises in the Vindhyapáda (Satpura range), does not appear to be correct.
KALSI	...	Srughna in the Jaunsár district on the east of Sirmur.
KALUHÁ	...	Same as *Kalhuá.*
KAMBAY	...	Stambha-tirtha in Guzerát.
KAMPIL	...	Kámpilya, twenty-eight miles north-east of Fathgarh in the district of Farrukhabad, N.-W. P. It was the capital of South Panchála, the king of which was Drupada, the father of Draupadi of the Mahábhárat. It was the birth-place of the celebrated astronomer Varáhamihira, (*Brihat-Játaka*).

MODERN NAMES.	ANCIENT NAMES OR SITUATION.
KÁMPTÁNÁTH-GIRI ...	Chitrakuta in Bundelkhand on the river Pisani, twelve miles from Márkund and fifty miles south-east of Banda. Rámachandra resided here for some time while on his way to the Dandakáranya.
KÁMPUR ...	Kanikshapura, ten miles to the south of Srinagar in Kásmir, founded by Kaniksha, king of Kásmir.
KANARAK ...	1. Arkakshetra, 2. Padmakshetra, nineteen miles north-west of Puri in Orissa. It contains a temple of the Sun, built by Languliya Narsinha, the seventh king of the Gangávansi dynasty, who reigned from 1237 to 1282 A. D.
KANE ...	1. The river Karnávati, 2. the Kriyána, in Bundelkhand.
KANGRA ...	1. Nagarakota, 2. Bhimanagara on the Ravi-Bánganga river. It was the old capital of Kuluta.
KANKAN ...	1. Parasuráma-kshetra. 2. It was part of Aparántaka : Kankan and Malabar formed the ancient Aparántaka.
KANKHAL ...	See *Hardwar*.
KANOUJ ...	1. Kányakubja, 2. Gádhipura, 3. Kusamapura, 4. Kusasthala, 5. Mahodaya, on the river Káli, a branch of the Ganges. After the Andhra-bhrityas of Pataliputra, the Guptas (from Sri or Rájá Gupta to Mahendra, a minor son of Skanda Gupta) rose into power and reigned at Kanouj (319 to 465 A. D.). From Chandra Gupta I, the third king

MODERN NAMES.	ANCIENT NAMES OR SITUATION.
	of the dynasty, to Skanda Gupta, the period is sixty-five years from 401 to 465 A. D. They adopted a new era called the Gupta era in 319 A. D. (Fergusson). The Guptas were destroyed by the Hunas under Toraman and his son Mihirakula in the sixth century. Kanouj was the birth-place of Viswámitra of the Rámáyana. Siláditya II. or Harshavardhana (known as Sri Harsha in Sanskrit literature), who was the fourth king after Vikramáditya of Ujjaini, made Kanouj his capital and reigned from 610 to 650 A. D. (Max Müller). He was visited by Hiuen Tsiang in 636 A. D In his court flourished the celebrated writer Bánabhatta (called also Bhandin) —the author of the Kádamvari, Harsha-charita, and Ratnávali; Dhávaka—the real author of the Nágánanda; and Chandráditya who versified the Vessantara Játaka. The celebrated poet Bhavabhuti was in the court of Yasavarmana of Kanouj: he went to Kásmir with Lalitáditya (672 to 728 A. D.) after the conquest of Kanouj by the latter (*Rájatarangini*). Sriharsha wrote the Naishadha-charita at the request of Jayachandra, king of Kanouj, in the eleventh century.
KAPILADHÁRÁ ...	I. Kapila-ásrama, twenty-four miles to the south-west of Násik: it was the hermitage of Kapila Rishi. II. The first fall of the Nerbuda from the Amarakantaka mountain.

MODERN NAMES.	ANCIENT NAMES OR SITUATION.
KÁRÁBAGH ...	Kárápatha on the Indus, mentioned in the *Raghuvansa* as being the place where Lakshmana's son Chandraketu was placed as king by his uncle Rámachandra when he made a disposition of his kingdom before his death. Tavernier writes it as *Carabat*.
KARACHI ...	Karakalla in Scind.—Krokala of Megasthenes.
KARATOYA ...	1. The river Karotoyá, 2. the Sadánirá, which flows through the districts of Rungpur and Dinajpur. It formed the boundary between the kingdoms of Bengal and Kámarupa at the time of the Mahábhárat.
KARMANÁSÁ ...	The river is situated on the western limit of the district of Shahabad in Bengal, and forms the boundary between the province of Bengal and the North-Western Provinces. Its water is considered to be polluted by the Hindus, being associated with the sins of Trisanku of the Rámáyana.
KARNA-PRAYÁGA	At the confluence of the Alakànandà and Pindar rivers. It is one of the five (Pancha) Prayágas.
KÁRON ...	Káma-ásrama, eight miles to the north of Korantedi in the district of Balia in the North-Western Provinces. Mahádeo is said to have destroyed Madana, the god of love, at this place with the fire of the third eye in his forehea .

MODERN NAMES.		ANCIENT NAMES OR SITUATION.
KARRA	...	Karkotaka-nagara, forty-one miles north-west of Allahabad. It is one of the 52 Pithas.
KÁRTTIKA-SWÁMI	...	Same as *Kumára-swámi.*
KASAI	...	The river Kansávati in Bengal.
KASIA	...	Kusinagara, thirty-five miles to the east of Gorakhpur on the old channel of the Hiranyavati or Chhota Gandak. It was at Kusinagara that Buddha died. The ashes of Buddha's funeral pyre were enshrined in a stupa at Barhi, now called Moriyanagar, in the Nyágrodha forest, visited by Hiuen Tsiang.
KÁSMIR	...	Kásyapapura : the hermitage of Rishi Kásyapa was on the Hari mountain, three miles from Srinagar.
KASUR	...	Kusávati, thirty-two miles to the south-east of Lahore, said to have been founded by Kusa, son of Rámachandra.
KATAK	...	Váránasi-Kataka in Orissa, at the confluence of the Mahánadi and Kátjuri, founded by Nripa Kesari, who reigned between 941 to 953 A. D.
KATHIWAR	..	The southern portion of Kathiwar was called Prabhása, containing the celebrated temple of Somnáth, at a short distance from which was the spot where Krishna died.
KÁTMANDU	...	1. Káshthamandapa, 2. Kántipuri, the capital of Nepál.

MODERN NAMES.	ANCIENT NAMES OR SITUATION:
KATWA ...	Katadwipa in the district of Burdwan in Bengal.
KÁVERI ...	The river Arddhagangá.
KEDÁR ...	The celebrated temple of Kedáranátha is situated in the Rudra-Himalaya in Gurwal below the peak of Mahápantha on the west of Badrinath. The worship of Mahádeo Kedáranátha is said to have been established by Arjuna, one of the five Pándavas. The river Káli-Gangá rises at this place and joins the Alákánandá at Rudra-Prayága.
KESARIYA ...	Isalia of the Buddhists, thirty miles north of Besarh in the district of Mozaffarpur in the province of Bengal, where Buddha passed the eighteenth and nineteenth Wassos of his Buddha-hood.
KETAS ...	1. Sinhapura of the Mahábhárat, 2. Katáksha, a town in the Panjáb, sixteen miles from Pindi Dadan Khan on the north of the Salt Range. According to Hiuen Tsiang, the country of Sinhapura bordered on the Indus on its western side. It was conquered by Arjuna.
KHAIRA-DIH ...	Jamadagni-ásrama, thirty-six miles north-west of Balia: it is said to have been the residence of Rishi Jamadagni and the birth-place of his son Parasuráma. See *Zamania*.
KHANDES ...	Khandes, Southern Malwa and parts of Aurangabad formed the ancient country of Haihaya or Anupadesa, the kingdom

MODERN NAMES.	ANCIENT NAMES OR SITUATION.
	of the myriad-handed Kárttyaviryárjuna, who was killed by Parasuráma. Its capital was Máhishmati (modern Maheswar or Mahes) on the river Nerbuda, forty miles to the south of Indore.
KHEDA (KAIRA) ...	Khetaka of the Padma Purán between Ahmedabad and Khambay in Guzerát. It is the Kiecha of Hiuen Tsiang, which Cunningham has correctly restored to Kheta or Kheda, now called Kaira. Khetaka was situated on a small river called Vetravati near its junction with the Sábhramati (Sabarmati). Julien renders Kiecha by Khacha or Kachchha.
KHIRAGRAMA ...	Twenty miles to the north of Burdwan. It is one of the 52 Pithas.
KISKINDHYA ...	A small hamlet on the north bank of the river Tungabhadra, not far from Anagandi. It was the ancient Kishkindhyá of the Rámáyana, where Rámchandra killed Báli, the king of the monkeys.
KIUNLUN RANGE	Same as *Kailas.*
KOH .	The river Kutikoshtika of the Rámáyana, a small affluent of the Ramaganga in Oudh.
KOLAPUR ...	1. Kolhápura, 2. Agastya-ásrama, the hermitage of Rishi Agastya, in the province of Bombay.
KOLLUR ...	Gani on the river Krishna, celebrated for its diamond mine (Tavernier). Gani is evidently the corruption of *Khani* (mine).

MODERN NAMES.	ANCIENT NAMES OR SITUATION.
KONDAVIR ...	1. Kundinapura, 2. Bidarbhanagara, the ancient capital of Bidarbha, and the birth-place of Rukmini, wife of Krishna, 3. Bhimapura. Cunningham identifies it also with Kusávati, but this identification is doubtful. Another Kondavir is mentioned by Tavernier, at present called Konavaidu, in the province of Madras, not far from Guntur: it was built in the twelfth century by a king of Orissa. Kondavir is the same as Kundapura of Dowson, forty miles east of Amaravati in Central India.
KONKONA ...	Same as *Kankan*.
KORUR ...	Between Multan and Loni, where Vikramáditya, king of Ujjaini, defeated the Sakas in a decisive battle in 533 A. D.,—the date of this battle is supposed to have given rise to the Samvat era.
KOSÁM ...	1. Kausámbi, 2. Kosambinagara, 3. Vatsya-pattana, about thirty miles to the west of Allahabad: it was the capital of Vatsya-desa, the kingdom of Ràjá Udayana. Harsha Deva places his scene of the *Ratnávali* at this place.
KOSILA ...	The river Kutiká or Kutilá of the Rámáyana, the eastern tributary of the Ramaganga in Oudh.
KOTAH ...	The district of Kotah in Rajputana appears to have been the ancient Seka, which was conquered by Sahadeva (*Mahábhárat*). Yule, however, identifies Sèka

	with the country around Jhajpur on the Banas to the south-east of Ajmir.
KOTALGARH ...	Sonitapura of the *Harivansa*, where Ushá was abducted by Aniruddha, the grandson of Krishna. See *Vána Rájá's gar*.
KOTA-TIRTHA ...	In Kálanjara.
KOTESAR ...	1. Kotiswara, 2. Kachchheswara, the capital of Kachchha (Kutch) on the river Kori, a branch of the Indus
KOTI-TIRTHA ...	I. In Mathura. II. A sacred tank in Gokarna.
KOTWAL ...	Kántipuri, twenty miles north of Gawalior.
KRISHNA ...	1. The river Krishná, 2. the Krishnaveni, 3. the Krishnavenwá, 4. the Benwá, 5. the Veni, 6. the Biná, 7. the Tynna of the Greeks.
KUARI ...	The river Kumári in the Gawalior State : it joins the river Sindh near its junction with the Jamuna.
KULU ...	1. Kuluta, 2. Koluka in the upper valley of the Beas. Its capital was Nagarakota.
KUMÁRA-SWÁMI	Is about one hundred and twenty miles to the south-east of Tirupati in the province of Madras.
KUMBHACONUM	1. Kámakoshthi 2. Kumbhaghonum in the province of Madras. It was the ancient capital of Chola.

MODERN NAMES.	ANCIENT NAMES OR SITUATION.
KUNDAPURA ...	1. Kundinapura, 2. Kundinanagara, 3. Bidarbhanagara, 4. Bhimapura, forty miles east of Amarávati in Central India. Same as *Kondavir*.
KURKIHAR ...	Kukkutapádagiri in the district of Gayá, where the Buddhist saint Mahá-Kasyapa died.
KUSHÁN ...	Kapisá, ten miles west of Opian on the declivity of the Hindu-Kush.
KUSI ...	The river Kausiki in Bengal. Its confluence with the Ganges was known as the Kausiki Tirtha or Kausiki-sangama.

L

LÁHARI-BANDAR	The ruins of Dewala,—the "Metamorphosed city" as it has been called,—are situated at a very short distance to the north of Láhari-bandar or Lári-bandar in Scind: in fact, Láhari-bandar was built with the ruins from Dewala (Cunningham).
LAHOR ...	Sálatura, the birth-place of Pánini, the celebrated grammarian. The village is situated at a distance of about sixteen miles to the north-east of Attok.
LAHORE ...	1. Lavakota, 2. Lavavára in the Panjab. It was founded by Lava, son of Rámachandra of the Rámáyana.
LAMGHAN ...	1. Lampáká, 2. Murandá on the northern bank of the Kábul river.

MODERN NAMES.	ANCIENT NAMES OR SITUATION.
LITTLE-GANDAK	Same as *Chhota-Gandak*.
LITTLE THIBET	Bolor. Little Thibet is also called Baltistan and Chitral. Its capital was Skardu.
LOMASGIR-HILL	Lomasa-ásrama, the hermitage of Lomasa Rishi: it is four miles north-east of Rájauli in the sub-division of Nowadah in the district of Gayá.
LOONI ...	The river Lánguli in Rájputáná.

M

MADAWAR ...	1. Matipura in Western Rohilkhand, visited by Hiuen Tsiang, 2. Pralamba of the Rámáyaná.
MADHYÁRJUNA...	Sixteen miles west of Tranquebar.
MADURA ...	1. Mathurá, 2. Dakshina-Mathura, 3. Minákshi, in the province of Madras. It was the capital of Pándya. The districts of Madura and Tinnivelly formed the ancient Pándya or Pándu. It is one of the 52 Pithas where Sati's eyes are said to have fallen.
MAHÁBALIPUR ...	Banapura on the Coromandal Coast. The "raths" of Mababalipur are the true representation of ancient Buddhist viharas or monasteries.
MAHABANA ...	A town about six miles from Mathura across the Jamuna. Gokul, in which Krishna was reared up during his infancy,

MODERN NAMES.	ANCIENT NAMES OR SITUATION.
	was the waterside suburb of Mahabana. Mahabana was the ancient Braja, and the Klisoboras of the Greeks. It was sacked by Mahmud of Ghazni as the "fort of Raja Kulchand" (see *Gokul.*)
MAHANADI ...	1. The river Chitrapalá, 2 the Chitrotpalá, 3. the Mahánadi in Orissa.
MANENDRA-MÁLI HILLS ...	The Mahendra hills of Ganjam, where Parasuráma retired after he was defeated by Ráma. The hills included the Eastern Ghâts.
MAHES ...	Same as *Maheswar*.
MAHESWAR ...	Máhishmati on the right bank of the Nerbuda, forty miles to the south of Indore. It was the capital of Haihaya or Anupadesa, the kingdom of the myriad-handed Kárttyavirjárjuna of the Puráns.
MAHI ...	I. 1. The river Mahati (*Váyu Purán*), 2. the Mahi (*Márkandeya Purán*) in Malwa. II. Mahendra in the Malabar coast.
MAHOBA ...	Mahotsava-nagara in Bundelkhand (Cunningham).
MALABAR ...	1. Mallára-desa, 2. part of Aparántaka : Malabar and Konkona formed the ancient Aparántaka, 3. Malabar, Travancore and Canara formed the ancient Kerala, called also Ugra.
MALABAR COAST	1. Kerala, 2. Ugra (see *Malabar*).

MODERN NAMES.	ANCIENT NAMES OR SITUATION.
MALABAR GHATS	1. Malaya-giri, 2. Chandana-giri : the southern portion of the Western Gháts, south of the river Kaveri.
MÁLINI ...	1. Same as the river *Chuka* in Oudh, which flows between the ancient countries called Pralamba and Aparatála, and falls into the river Ghágra (Saraju) fifty miles above Ajodhya. The hermitage of Kanwa, the adoptive father of the celebrated Sakuntalá, was situated on the bank of this river. 2. Erineses of Megasthenes.
MALKHEAD ...	Mányakshetra on the river Krishna.
MALL ...	Upamallaka.
MALWA ...	1. Málava, 2. Avanti. Its capitals were Ujjaini and Dháránagara.
MANÁL ...	A village near Badrinath in Gurwal. It was the hermitage of Rishi Vyása, the author of the Mahábharat.
MÁNAS-SAROVAR	The lake Mánasa-sarovara, 2. Mánasa is situated at the foot of that part of the Kailása range which is called Baidyuta-parvata.
MANBHUM ...	The western portion of the district of Manbhum in the province of Bengal appertained to the ancient country of Malla-desa.
MANDÁKINI ...	I. Same as the river *Káli-nadi*. II. The river Paisuni (ancient Payoshni) which flows by the side of Chitrakuta in

MODERN NAMES.	ANCIENT NAMES OR SITUATION.
	Bundelkhand: it was created by Anusuyá, the wife of Rishi Atri and daughter of Daksha, to avert the effect of a drought of ten years.
MANDÁRAGIRI ...	A hill in the Bánká sub-division of Bhágalpur in Bengal, two or three miles from Bansi. The gods are said to have churned the ocean with this hill as a churner.
MANDASOR ...	Dasapura on the Chambal in Malwa, about ninety-five miles south-east of Udayapur.
MANGALÁ-GOURI	One of the 52 Pithas, in Gaya.
MANGILA-PATTANA. ...	Pratishthána, thirty-eight miles south-west of Aurangabad. It was the capital of Rájá Sáliváhana, king of Maháráshtra.
MANGLORA ...	1. Mangala, 2. Mangali, 3. Mangalapura on the Swat river. It was the capital of Udyána.
MANIKALYA ...	Mánikapura in the Panjab, celebrated for its Buddhist topes where Buddha in a former birth gave his body to feed a starving tiger.
MANIKARNIKÁ ...	Brahmanála in Benares.
MÁNIKPATTAN ...	Manipura of the Mahábhárat, a seaport at the mouth of the lake Chilka. It was once the capital of Kalinga. The situation of the capital of Kalinga as

MODERN NAMES.	ANCIENT NAMES OR SITUATION.
	described in the Mahábhárat and the Raghuvansa and also the name accord with those of Mánikpattan.
MÁRÁTTA COUNTRY ...	Máhárásbtra, the boundaries of which in the seventh century were: Malwa on the north, Kosala and Andhra on the east, Konkona on the south, and the sea on the west. Its ancient capitals were Pratishthána, Kalyáni and Devagiri.
MARWAR ...	Mordua-desa in Rajputana: Gurjara of the seventh century.
MASAR ...	Mahásara, an ancient village six miles to the west of Arrah in the district of Shahabad in Bengal, visited by Hiuen Tsiang, at a very short distance from the Karisat station of the E. I. Railway. It now contains only two temples.
MATHURA ...	1. Madhupuri, 2. Surasena. It was founded by Satrughana, and was the birth-place of Krishna. Eighty miles all round Mathura was called the Vraja-Mandala.
MAURAWAN ...	Six miles east of Unao in Oudh. It is said to have been the capital of Mayuradhwaja of the Mahábhárat (Führer).
MÁYÁPUR ...	1. Máyápuri, 2. Mayura (see *Hardwar*).
MEGNA ...	1. The river Meghanáda, 2. the Meghaváhana in east Bengal.
MEWAR ...	Sákambhari in Rajputana.

MODERN NAMES.		ANCIENT NAMES OR SITUATION.
MHOW	...	Anupadesa in Malwa. Growse identifies Anupadesa with Vraja (*Mathura*, p. 310).
MIDNAPUR	...	The southern portion of Bengal, including the district of Midnapur, was the ancient Sumha.
MIKULA	...	1. The Mekala hills, 2. the Soma-parvata in which the rivers Narbuda and Sone have their source.
MINAGAR	...	In Scind: Pishenpopulo of Hiuen Tsiang, which is Vichawapura according to Julien, but which Reinaud restores to Vasmapura (Beal). Saminagara (Tod).
MIRAT	...	1. Mayaráshtra, 2. Mayarát, the residence of Maya Dánava, the father of Mandodari, the wife of Rávana.
MITHILÁ	...	1. Videha, 2. Tirabhukti, 3. Trihuta, 4. Janakapura, the capital of Rájá Janaka, the father of Sitá.
MOHWAR	...	The river Madhumati in Malwa, which rises near Ranod and falls into the Sindh about eight miles above Sonari. The river has been mentioned in Bhavabhuti's *Málati-Mádhava*.
MONG	...	Nikai or Nikœa of the Greeks on the Hydaspes in the Gujrat district, where the celebrated battle was fought between Alexander the Great and Porus (Puru).
MONGHIR	...	1. Mudgalagiri from Mudgalaputra, a disciple of Buddha, 2. Mudga-giri (a contraction of Mudgala-giri), 3. Modágiri, 4. Hiranyaparvata of Hiuen Tsiang.

MODERN NAMES.	ANCIENT NAMES OR SITUATION.
MUKTINATH ...	A celebrated place of pilgrimage situated in Thibet or north of Nepal on the Sapta-Gandaki range of the Himalaya, south of Sálagráma, not far from the source of the Gandak. The place is associated with the legend of Tulsi and Náráyana, and a temple of the latter exists at this place: hence the Gandak is called the Náráyani.
MULTAN ...	1. Mulasthánapura, 2. Mauli-snána (*Padma Purán*), 3. Prahládapuri, where Náráyana incarnated as Nrisinha and killed the Asura Hiranyakasipu, the father of Prahláda. It was the capital of Malladesa, or the country of the Mallis of Alexander's historians, which was given to Lakshmana's son Angada by his uncle Rámachandra, when the latter made a disposition of his kingdom before his death.
MUNDORE ...	Same as *Madawar*.
MURG ...	Same as *Mong*.
MUZAFFARNAGAR	Khándava-vana of the Mahábhárat, north of Mirat: it is one of the stations of the North-Western Railway. Arjuna appeased the hunger of Agni, the god of fire, at this place.
MYSORE ..	1. Mahishaka, 2. Maheswara, 3. Vanavási of the Buddhist period.

N.

NANDA-PRAYÁGA	At the confluence of the Alakánandá and Nandákini, a small river. It is one of the five (Pancha) Prayágas.

MODERN NAMES.	ANCIENT NAMES OR SITUATION.
NARWAR ...	1. Nishadha, 2. Nalapura, forty miles south-west of Gwaliar. It was the capital of Rájá Nala of the story of Nala-Damayanti of the Puráns.
NASIK ...	Panchavati-vana on the Godavari, where Sitá was abducted by Rávana, king of Lanká. The name of Nasik is evidently derived from the circumstance of Surpanaká's nose having been cut at this place by Lakshmana.
NATHADWAR ...	Siarh on the Banas, twenty-two miles north-east of Udayapur in Mewar. It contains the celebrated original image of Kesava Deva removed by Rana Ráj Singh from Mathura in anticipation of Aurangzeb's raid.
NAWAL ...	Navadevakula, thirty-three miles north-west of Unao near Bangarmau in Oudh, visited by Hiuen Tsiang (Führer).
NEGAPATAM ...	1. Uragapura, 2. Nágapattana, the capital of Pándu or Pándya, in the province of Madras.
NERBUDA ...	1. The river Narmadá, 2. the Muralá, 3. the Purva-Gangá, 4. the Revá. It rises in the Amarakantaka mountain.
NIGAMBOD-GHAT	Nigambodha-tirtha of the Padma Purán in Old Delhi (Indraprastha).
NIGLIVA ...	In the Nepalese Terai, north of Gorakhpur and thirty-eight miles north-west of the Uska station of the Bengal and North-Western Railway. It has been identified by Dr. Führer with Kapila-

MODERN NAMES.	ANCIENT NAMES OR SITUATION.
	vastu, the birth-place of Buddha. The ruins of Kapilavastu lie eight miles north-west of Paderia, which has been identified with the Lumbini garden, where Buddha was born.
NILAKANTHA ...	A celebrated place of pilgrimage containing the temple of Nilakantha Mahádeo to the north of Katmandu in Nepal.
NILGIRI ...	The Nila Parvata or Niláchala in the district of Puri in Orissa.
NIMKHÁRVAN ...	Naimisháranya, twenty-four miles from the Sandila station of the Oudh and Rohilkhand Railway, and twenty miles from Sitapur, on the left bank of the Gumti. It was the abode of sixty-thousand Rishis: many of the Puráns were written at this place.
NIMSAR ...	Same as *Nimkhàrvan*.
NIZAM'S STATE	1. Andhra, 2. Tailanga, 3. Tri-Kalinga between the Godavari and the Krishna.
NORTHERN CIRCARS ...	The southern portion of the Northern Circars between the Chikakol river and the Godavari was called Mohana-desa; the northern portion was part of Kalinga.
NUDDEA ...	Navadwipa in Bengal, the birth-place of Chaitanya. It was the last Hindu capital of Bengal, conquered by Bakhtiar Khiliji in 1203. To the north-east of the present Navadwipa, at the distance

MODERN NAMES ANCIENT NAMES OR SITUATION.

of about a mile, are the ruins of Ballála Sena's palace, and there is also a tank of Ballála Sena called Balláladighi.

NUNDGAON ... Nandigráma of the Rámayána in Oudh where Bharata resided during the exile of Rámachandra.

NYSATTA ... Nysa of the Greeks on the northern bank cf the Kabul river, about two leagues below Hashtanagar.

O.

OHIND ... Udakhanda on the right bank of the Indus in the Peshawur division of the Panjab.

OMKÁRNATH ... Amateswara, near Mandaleswara, which is five miles to the east of Mahes (the ancient Máhishmati) on the bank of the Nerbuda. It is one of the twelve great Lingas of Mahádeo.

OPIAN ... Hupian, twenty-seven miles to the north of Kábul.

ORISSA ... 1. Udra, 2. Odra, 3. Utkala.

OUDH ... 1. Ayodhyá, the kingdom of Ráma, 2. Kosala: it was divided into Uttara and Dakshina Kosala, 3. Sáketa, 4. Setiká, 5. Visákhá, 6. the town Ayodhyá.

OUJEIN ... 1. Ujjaini, 2. Avantipura. It was the capital of Vikramáditya (II) the Great (515 to 550 A. D.), who revived Hinduism and introduced Siva-worship. His victory cver the Sakas in 533 A. D. gave rise to the Samvat era. In his court

MODERN NAMES. ANCIENT NAMES OR SITUATION.

flourished the celebrated poet Kálidása, the author of the Sakuntalá; Amara Sinha, the author of the Amara-Kosha; Varáha-mihira, the author of the Brihat-Játaka; Bararuchi (called also Kátyáyana), the author of the Várttika and Prákrita-prakása; Ghatakarpara, the author of the Yamaka-kávya; Dhanwantari, the author of the Briddha Susruta Sanhitá; Kshapanaka (also called Dinnágácharya—a disciple of the Buddhist patriarch Basubandhu), the commentator of the Nyáya-sutras of Gautama; Sanku; and Betálabhatta, the chronicler. They were called the "nine gems" of the court of Vikramáditya. Oujein contains the celebrated temple of the Mahádeva called Mahákála of the Purâns and Kálapriyanátha of the dramas. On the northern side of the town is situated the hermitage of Sandipana Muni, where Krishna and Balaráma were educated. Bhatrihari's cave is about two miles to the north of the town on the bank of the Sipra. The Bhairava mountain near Oujein is one of the 52 Pithas, where Sati's upper lip is said to have fallen.

OXUS ... 1. The river Vakshu, 2. the Suchakshu, 3. the Chakshu.

P.

PADERIA ... A village in the Nepalese Terai, two miles north of Bhagabanpur. It has been identified with the Lumbini garden, where Buddha was born (see *Nigliva*).

MODERN NAMES.		ANCIENT NAMES OR SITUATION.
PAIN-GANGA	...	The river Nirvindhyá of the Puráns, a tributary of the Godavari.
PÁKPATTAN	...	Ayodhana in the Panjab.
PALITHANA	...	In Guzerát, situated at the foot of a mountain called Satrunjaya, to the south-west of Bhaonagar. It is one of the five hills sacred to the Jainas and contains a temple of Ádináth.
PALNI-HILLS	...	1. Sri-saila, 2. Rishabha-parvata, in the district of Madura (*Chaitanya-Charitámrita*)
PAMPA	...	A branch of the Tangabhadra. Mount Rishyamukha is situated on the eastern bank of this river, where Rámachandra met Hanumána and Sugriva for the first time. There is also a lake called Pampá-Sarovara near Kishkindhya (see *Kishkindhyá*).
PÁMPUR	...	Padmapura on the right bank of the Behat (Jhelum), eight miles to the south-east of Srinagar in Kasmir. It is celebrated for its cultivation of *Kunkuma* or saffron *(crocus sativus)*, which was largely used as a cosmetic by the ladies of ancient India.
PANCHÁNA	...	1. The river Nandá, 2. the Panchánandá, which flows through the districts of Gayá and Pátná. It flows by the side of Ratna-giri, called also Hemakuta or Rishabha-giri, one of the five hills of Rajgir, where Rishabha Rishi performed asceticism. Rishabha Rishi's image is

MODERN NAMES.	ANCIENT NAMES OR SITUATION.
	sculptured in the Baibhára-giri near the Sonabhándára cave.
PANDERPUR ...	Pándupura on the river Bhima in the district of Sholapur in the province of Bombay. It contains the celebrated temple of Bithalnáth or Bithoba Deva, an image of Krishna. Krishna is said to have visited this place with Rukmini to see Pundarika, who was celebrated for his filial affection.
PANDRITAN ...	Puránádhishthána, the ancient capital of Kásmir, eight miles to the east of Srinagar.
PÁNDUA ...	I. Pundravardhana, the ancient capital of Bengal, six miles north of Malda. II. Pradyumna-nagara in the district of Hugli in Bengal.
PANIPA ...	Pániprastha.
PANJAB ...	1. Panchanada, 2. Áratta, 3. Takka-desa (Hiuen Tsiang), the country of the five rivers Satadru (Sutlej), Vipásá (Beas), Irávati (Rávi), Chandrabhágá (Chenab) and Vitastá (Jhelum).
PANJSHIR ...	Julien supposes that Panjshir and Tagao valleys in the north border of Kohistan comprised the ancient district of Kapisá.
PÁRASNATH HILL ...	1. Sameta-sekhara, 3. Malla-parvata, 3. Mount Maleus of the Greeks in the district of Hazaribagh in Bengal. It is one of the five hills sacred to the Jainas.

MODERN NAMES.	ANCIENT NAMES OR SITUATION.
PARASURAMA-PURA ...	Twelve miles south-east of Patti in the district of Pratapgarh in Oudh. It is one of the 52 Pithas.
PÁRBATI ...	1. The river Párá, 2. the Párávati which falls into the river Sindh in Malwa near Vijayanagara, the ancient Padmávati.
PASUPATINÁTH	A celebrated temple of Mahádeo in Nepal, associated with the story of the fowler and the god.
PATNA ...	1. Pátaliputra, 2. Kusamapura, 3. Pushpapura, the capital of Magadha, where Udáyi or Udayáswa, the grandson of Ajátasatru (contemporary of Buddha), removed the seat of government from Rájagriha. The dynasties from Chandragupta which reigned at Pátaliputra are: the Mauryas from Chandragupta to Brihadratha (325 to 195 B. C.): in the seventeenth year of the reign of Asoka (276 to 240 B. C.), the grandson of Chandragupta, the third Buddhist synod was held at Pátaliputra under the presidency of Mudgaliputra Tissa; the Sungas from Pushpamitra to Devabhuti (188 to 76 B. C.); the Kanwas from Vasudeva to Susarman (76 to 31 B. C.); the Andhra-bhrityas (Satakarnis or Satavábanas of the inscriptions) from Sipraka to Gautamiputra (31 B. C. to 312 A. D.); the Vasithiputras from Puliman, son of Gautamiputra, to Pulomáchi (333 to 429 A. D.). Pátaliputra was the birth-place of the celebrated astrono-

MODERN NAMES.	ANCIENT NAMES OR SITUATION.
	mer Áryabhatta, the author of the *Surya-siddhánta*, who was born in 554 A. D.
PATTAN ...	I. 1. Anahila-pattana, 2. Anhulwara-pattana, in Guzerát. II. 1. Mangila-pattana, 2. Sáliváhanapura, thirty-eight miles south-west of Aurangabad: it was the capital of Sáliváhana.
PAUMBEN PASSAGE ...	Dhanu-tirtha between India and Ceylon, which was caused by Lakshmana piercing the water with his bow.
PEGU ...	1. Ramanya, 2. Aramana in Burma.
PEHOA ...	Prithudaka, where the celebrated Brahmayoni-tirtha is situated: fourteen miles to the west of Thaneswar.
PENNAR ...	The river Pinákini in the province of Madras.
PERSIA ...	Párasya: its capital was Surasthána according to Hiuen Tsiang.
PESHAWUR ...	Purushapura, the capital of Gándhára (see *Cabul Valley*).
PHALGU ...	1. The river Mahánadi of the Mahábhárat, on which Gaya is situated, 2. the Lilájana, 3. the Nilájana, 4. the Nairanjana, 5. the Niranjana, 6. the Nilanchana, of the Buddhists.
PISANI ...	1. The river Payoswini, 2. the Paisuni, 3. the Mandákini, which flows by the side of Chitrakuta in Bundelkhand.
POREBUNDER ...	Sudámápuri in Guzerát.

MODERN NAMES.		ANCIENT NAMES OR SITUATION.
PRANAHITA	...	1. The river Mahásála, 2. the Maisolus of the Greeks, 3. the Pranitá, the united stream of the rivers Wardhá and Waingangá in Central India.
PUHAT	...	Punach in Kasmir.
PUNDERPUR	...	Same as *Panderpur.*
PUNPUN	...	The river Punahpuna, a tributary of the Ganges in the district of Patna in Bengal.
PURI	...	1. Purushottama-kshetra, 2. Srikshetra, 3. Dantapura (Hunter and Fergusson), 4. Charitrapura, in Orissa. The temple of Jagannáth was built by Ananga Bhima Deo of the Gangá dynasty in 1198 A. D.
PURNÁ	...	1. The river Payoshni, 2. the Krathakaisika in Berar.
PURNEA	...	Kausikikachchha.
PURTI	...	The river Payoshni in Travancore (*J. B. T. S.*, Vol. V).
PUSHKAR	...	1. The Pushkara lake, 2. Brahmatirtha, six miles from Ajmir.
PYRI	...	The river Pretoddhárini which joins the Mahánadi at Raju.

R

RAILÁ	...	1. Ráhugráma, 2. Ashtábakra-ásrama, the hermitage of Rishi Ashtábakra, ten miles from Hardwar.

MODERN NAMES.	ANCIENT NAMES OR SITUATION.
RÁJAGIRI ...	Rájagriha of the Rámáyana on the north bank of the Beas. It was the capital of the Aswapatis.
RÁJAMAHENDRI	1. Dantapura (Cunningham and Mc-Crindle), 2. Vidyánagara on the Godavari, founded by Mahendra Deva. It was the capital of the Chalukya kings (eastern branch) from Kubja Vishnu Vardhana to Vira Deva Kulottunga (7th to 12th century).
RAJAURI ...	Rájapuri, south of Kásmir and south-east of Punach.
RÁJGIR ...	1. Girivrajapura of the Mahábhárat, 2. Rájagriha of the Buddhist annals, 3. Kuságárapura, in the district of Patna, was the capital of Magadha till the seat of government was removed to Pátaliputra (Patna). It was the abode of Jarásandha, king of Magadha. Buddha lived at Rajgir in the Venuvana garden presented to him by Rájá Bimbasara. The first Buddhist synod was held under the presidency of Mahá-Kásyapa shortly after Buddha's death in a hall built by Ajátasatru in front of the Satapanni cave by the side of the Vaibhara mountain. The Sisunága dynasty from Sisunága to the seven Nandas reigned at Girivrajapura from 685 to 325 B.C.; the seat of government was removed to Pátaliputra by Udayàswa who reigned from 519 to 503 B. C. Kálásoka, the eleventh king of this dynasty, in whose reign the second Buddhist synod was held in 443 B. C. at

MODERN NAMES.	ANCIENT NAMES OR SITUATION.
	Vaisali under the presidency of Revata, reigned from 453 to 425 B. C. (Fergusson).
RÁJMAHAL HILLS	1. Kakshivata, 2. Sushuni, in Bengal.
RÁJSHÁHI ...	Varendra in Bengal.
RÁMAHRAD ...	A tank in Tháneswar, sacred to Parasuráma.
RÀMESWARA-SANGAMA ...	The confluence of the river Banas with the Chambal in Rajputana.
RÁM-GANGÁ ...	1. The river Suvámá, 2. the Uttaragá, 3. the Uttánika of the Rámáyana in Oudh.
RÁMNAGAR ...	I. 1. Ahichchhatrapura, 2. Ahikshetra, 3. Ádikota, 4. Ahichhatra, the capital of North Panchála in Rohilkhand, twenty miles west of Bareli. There is still a place called Ahichhatrapura near Rámnagar. II. Vyásakási, opposite to Benares across the Ganges.
RÁMPÁLA ...	Ballála-bári, the capital of Ballála Sena, king of Bengal, about two miles from Munshiganj at Vikrampur in the district of Dacca.
RAMTEGE ...	Same as *Ramtek*.
RAMTEK ...	1. Rámagiri, 2. Sambuka-ásrama, the hermitage of the Sudra Sambuka of the Rámáyana, north of Nagpur in Central India.

MODERN NAMES.	ANCIENT NAMES OR SITUATION.
RÁNGÁMÁTI ...	1. Karna-Suvarna, 2. Kánsoná, on the right bank of the Bhágirathi, four miles below Berhampur in the district of Murshidabad in Bengal. It was the capital of Ádisura, king of Bengal
RANIGHAT ...	Aornos of the Greeks in the Panjab, about sixteen miles north-west of Ohind.
RATANPUR ...	Ratnapura, the capital of Dakshina-Kosala or Gandwana.
RATNAGIRI ...	1. Rishigiri, 2. Isigili of the Buddhists, 3. Rishabhagiri, 4. Hemakuta, one of the five hills of Rajgir in the district of Patna.
RÁVI	1. The river Irávati, 2. the Airávati, 3. the Parushni, 4. the Marudvriddha, 5. the Hydraotes of the Greeks, in the Panjab.
RAWANHRAD ...	1. The lake Rávana-hrada, 2. Kusávána-hrada of the Mahábhárat, 3. Anavatapta, 4. Anavatatta of the Buddhists.
RECHNA-DOAB ...	Between the Chenab and the Rávi in the Panjab. It comprised Madra-desa, called also Bálhika, the capital of which was Sákala.
REVELGANJ ...	Gautama-ásrama, near Chapra in Bengal: the hermitage of Gautama is situated at a place called Godnà, but the Rámáyana places the hermitage of the Rishi at a short distance from Janakpur in Tirhut. See *Godna*.

MODERN NAMES.		ANCIENT NAMES OR SITUATION.
RINTAMBUR	...	Rantipura on the Chambal in Rajputana. It was the residence of Ranti Deva alluded to by Kálidása in his *Meghaduta*. His sacrifice of cows brought into existence the river Charmanavati, on which the town is situated.
RISHIKUILA	...	1. The river Rishikulyá, 2. the Haimavati, on which Ganjam is situated. It rises in the Mahendra hills.
RISHYAMUKHA		It was on this mountain that Sugriva dwelt after he fled from Kishkindhyá. It is eight miles from the Anagandi hills on the Tungabhadra.
ROÁLSAR	...	About sixty-four miles to the north-west of Jwálámukhi: it is said to contain seven miraculously moving hills, and consequently it is a place of pilgrimage.
ROHILKHAND	...	Panchála: it was divided into North and South Panchála. The capital of North Panchála was Ahichchhatra (Ramnagar), and that of South Panchála was Kámpilya (Kampil). Drupada of the Mahábhárat was king of South Panchála.
ROHTAK	...	Rohitaka, forty-two miles north-west of Delhi.
ROHTAS	...	Rohita in the district of Shahabad in Bengal, thirty miles south of Sásiram. It is said to have been founded by Rohitáswa, son of Harisachandra of the Rámáyana and Márkandeya Purán.

MODERN NAMES.	ANCIENT NAMES OR SITUATION.
ROHTÁS HILLS...	1. Mauli, 2. Kimmritya, in the sub-division of Sásiram in the district of Shahabad. Same as *Kaimur hills*.
RUDRA-HIMA-LAYA ...	The part of the Rudra-Himalaya range in Gurwal, which is to the north-east of Badrinath, is called Gandhamádana. The portion of the Rudra-Himalaya where the Ganges has its source is called Sumeru. See *Gangotri*.
RUDRA-PRAYÁGA	At the confluence of the Alakánandá and Káligangá (Mandákini). It is one of the five (Pancha) Prayágas.

S.

SABARMATI ...	1. The river Sábhramati (*Padma Purán*), 2. the Sarávati, 3. the Kritavati, 4. the Chandaná, 5. the Girikarniká, 6. the Kásyapi-Gangá, in Guzerat.
SAGOR ...	The district of Sagor and the western portion of Bundelkhand formed the ancient Pulinda-desa.
SAHARANPUR ...	The district of Saharanpur appertained to the ancient Kulinda-desa.
SÁHET-MÁHET...	1. Srávasti, 2. Sarávati, 3. Sabathapura, 4. Dharmapattana, 5. Chandriká-puri, being the birth-place of Chandra-prabhá-náth, one of the Tirthankars of the Jainas. It is situated on the river Rápti in Oudh, fifty-eight miles north of

MODERN NAMES.	ANCIENT NAMES OR SITUATION.
	Ayodhyá and forty-two miles north of Gonda. It was the capital of North Kosala. Buddha lived here for twenty-five years.
SAI	The river Syandika of the Rámáyana, a branch of the Gumti in Oudh.
SAILA-GIRI ...	To the north-east of the old town of Rajgir, and to the south-east of the new town of Rajgir: it was the Gridhrakuta of the Buddhist annals—the Vulture peak of Fa Hian and Hiuen Tsiang.
SÁLAGRÁMA ...	Near the source of the river Gandak in the Sapta-Gandaki range of the Himalaya in the southern boundary of Central Thibet. It was the hermitage of Bharata and Pulaha. From the name of this place, the Gandak is called Sálagrámi.
SALSETTE ...	The island of Perimuda,—the Perimula of the Greeks, near Bombay. It derived its sanctity from a tooth of Buddha, which was enshrined there at the beginning of the fourth century.
SAMBHÁRA LAKE	Sákambhari in Rajputana.
SANGLAWALA-TIBA ...	1. Sákala, 2. Sánkala, the capital of Madra-desa, on the Apagá river west of the Rávi in the Pánjab.
SANKARA-TIRTHA	In Nepal immediately below the town of Patan at the confluence of the Bách-mati and the Manimati rivers.

MODERN NAMES.		ANCIENT NAMES OR SITUATION.
SANKISA	...	1. Sánkásya, 2. Kapitha on the river Ikshumati (now called Káli-nadi), twenty-three miles west of Fathgarh in the district of Farrakhabad.
SANKISA-BASANTAPUR	...	Same as *Sankisa*.
SARAI AGHAT	...	Agastya-ásrama, the hermitage of Agastya, forty-three miles south-west of Itah in the Itah district.
SARASWATI		The river rises in the hills in Sirmur and emerges into the plains at Ád-Badri or Ádi-tirtha. It lost itself in the sand at a place called Chamasodbheda, which is esteemed sacred by the Hindus.
SARIKKUL	..	Kabandha.
SARIKKUL LAKE		The lake Nágahrada,—the lake of the Great Pamir.
SÁRNÁTH	...	1. Sáranganátha, 2. Mrigadáva, 3. Rishipattana, 4 Isipatana of the Buddhists, six miles from Benares, where Buddha preached his first sermon after the attainment of Buddha-hood at Buddha-Gayá.
SARVANA	...	About twenty miles to the south-east of Unao in Oudh, where Dasaratha, king of Ayodhyá, killed Sarvana, the son of a blind Rishi.
SÁSIRAM	...	Sahansaráma in the district of Shahabad in Bengal.
SÁTGAON	...	Saptagráma, an ancient town of Bengal near Magra in the district of Hugli.

MODERN NAMES.	ANCIENT NAMES OR SITUATION.
SATPURA RANGE	1. Vindhyapáda-parvata (*Váyu Purán*), 2. Baidurya-parvata.
SEA (ARABIAN) ...	Paschimodadhi (*Padma Purán*).
SEHWAN ...	Sivisthána in Sindh, on the right bank of the Indus. It contains a ruined fortress of Bhatrihari, who is said to have reigned here after he abandoned Oujein on the death of his wife, Pingalá (Tod). Sindomana (Cunningham).
SEMAH ...	1. Semulapura (Sambhalpur ?) on the river Koel in the district of Palamu in the Chhota Nagpur division : Soumelpour of Tavernier, 2. Sambalaka of Ptolomey celebrated for its diamond mines (Ball).
SERINGAPATAM	Srirangapattana, on the Káveri, in Mysore.
SERINGHAM ...	1. Srirangam, 2. Srirangakshetra in the province of Madras.
SEVEN PAGODAS	1. Banapura, 2. Mahábalipura on the Coromandel Coast.
SEWALIK RANGE	Mainâka-giri.
SHAHABAD ...	The eastern portion of the district of Shahabad in Behar was called Karusha, and the western portion was called Malada.
SHAH-DHERI ...	1. Takshasila, 2. Taxila of the Greeks, one mile north of Kála-ká-serai, between Attock and Rawalpindi. The Kathá-saritságara places it on the Jhêlum.

MODERN NAMES.	ANCIENT NAMES OR SITUATION.
	Takshasila was founded by Taksha, son of Bharata and nephew of Rámachandra.
SHAH-KOTE ...	Aornos of the Greeks on Mount Mahában, situated on the western bank of the Indus.
SHECROH ...	In Lar, identified by Wilson with Hushkapura (see *Barámula*). Cunningham identifies Shecroh with Jushkapura, now called Zukur in Kásmir, four miles to the north of Srinagar.
SIAM ...	Dwáravati.
SIDDHAUR ...	Siddhapura, sixteen miles west of Bára-Banki in Oudh.
SINDH ...	I. The river Sindhu or Dakshina-Sindhu in Malwa. II. Sindhu-desa.
SINDH-SÁGAR DOAB ...	Between the Indus and the Jhelum. It comprised the ancient countries of Áyudha and Sauvira.
SINGBHUM ...	Kie-lo-na-su-fa-la-na of Hiuen Tsiang: it has been identified by Cunningham with Kirana-Suvarna (Singbhum) in the Chhota Nagpur division. Beal identifies it with Karna-Suvarna (Rángámáti) in the district of Murshidabad. Sasánka, king of Kirana-Suvarna, was a great persecutor of Buddhism: he destroyed the Bodhi tree at Buddha-Gaya (Hiuen Tsiang). It was the southern boundary of the kingdom of Magadha.

MODERN NAMES.	ANCIENT NAMES OR SITUATION.
SINGHÁRI-MAT...	Same as *Sringapura.*
SINGHESWARA...	1. Bibhándaka-ásramá, 2. Rishya-sringa-ásramá, four miles north of Madhepura in the district of Bhagalpur.
SINGRAUR ...	Sringaverapura on the Ganges, eighteen miles north-west of Allahabad. It was the residence of Guhaka Chandála of the Ramáyana, who was a friend of Daśaratha and Rámachandra.
SIPELER ...	A seaport near the mouth of the Krishná,—Sippará of Ptolemey. It has been identified by Dr. R. L. Mitra with Surpáraka (*Lalita-Vistara*), Cunningham identifies Surpáraka with Surat, but the *Chaitanya-charitámrita* places Surpáraka to the south of Kolhapur.
SIPRÁ ...	The Avanti-nadi in Malwa: Oujein stands on this river.
SIRHIND ...	1. Kurujángala of the Mahábhárat, 2. Sairindha-desa of the Purâns, 3. Srikantha-desa of the Buddhist period, 4. Satadru of Hiuen Tsiang, in the Panjab.
SITPUR ...	1. Siddhapura, 2. Kardama-ásrama and the birth-place of Kapila, 3. Bindusara in Guzerat, eighty-two miles from Ahmedabad.
SOMNÁTH ...	1. Prabhása, 2. Somatirtha, 3. Chandra-Prabhása of the Jainas, on the south of Guzerát. It is situated at the confluence of the three rivers Hariná, Kapilá

MODERN NAMES.	ANCIENT NAMES OR SITUATION.
	and Saraswati. On the south of the Saraswati (near Somnath) is situated that celebrated Pipal tree (*ficus religiosa*), below which was the scene of Krishna's death.
SONA-GIRI ...	1. Vrishabha-giri, one of the five hills of Rajgir, 2. Pandawo of the Buddhists.
SONÁRGÁON ...	Suvarnagráma in Bikrampur in the district of Dacca, situated on the opposite side of Munshiganj on the river Dhaleswari.
SONE ...	1. The river Hiranyaváhu, 2. the Erannoboas of the Greeks, 3. the Soná. It was the western boundary of Magadha.
SONEPAT ...	Sonaprastha: it was included in Kurukshetra.
SOONDA ...	Sudhápura in North Canara.
SORON ...	1. Sukara-kshetra, 2. Ukalakshetra, twenty-seven miles north-east of Itah in the N.-W. Provinces, where Hiranyáksha was slain by Vishnu in his incarnation as Varáha (boar). It contains a temple of Varáha-Lakshmi. It was at this place that Tulsi Dás, the celebrated Hindi poet, was reared up during his childhood by the Sanyási Nrisinha Dás, when deserted by his parents at Rájapuri in the district of Banda, where he was born in Sambat 1589.
SRINAGAR ...	Suryanagara in Kásmir, built by Pravara Sen in the sixth century.

MODERN NAMES.		ANCIENT NAMES OR SITUATION.
SRINGAPURA	...	Sringagiri in Cochin, where Sankarácharya established a sect called Bhárati (*J. B. T. S.*, Vol. V., p. 45).
SUGH	...	Srughna, near Kálsi, in the Jaunsár district, forty miles from Tháneswar and twenty miles to the north of Saharanpur.
SUJANAKOT	...	Sanchankot : Sha-chi of Fa Hian. It was the capital of Sáketa or Oudh, thirty-four miles north-west of Unao.
SUKRI-NADI	...	The Aparanandá, a small river which flows through the districts of Gaya and Patna, and falls into the Ganges.
SULTANGANJ	...	On the west of Bhagalpur (E. I. Railway): Janhu-ásrama : it was the hermitage of Jahnu Muni, from whom the Ganges (Gangá) is called Jáhnavi.
SULTANPUR	...	I. Támasavana monastery in the Panjab (Cunningham), where the last Buddhist synod was held in 78 A. D. by Kaniksha, king of Kásmir, under the presidency of Vasumitra. The date of this convocation gave rise to the Saka era. But Beal places Támasavana at the confluence of the Sutlej and the Beas. II. 1. Kusabhavanapura, 2. Kusapura in Oudh on the river Gumti. The town is said to have been founded by Kusa, son of Rámachandra, who removed his capital to this place for some time. It was visited by Hiuen Tsiang in the seventh century.
SURÁT	...	1. Suryapura (Prinsep), 2. Suráshtra.

k

MODERN NAMES.	ANCIENT NAMES OR SITUATION.
ṢUTLEJ ...	1. The river Satadru, 2. the Sitadru, 3. the Hesadrus of the Greeks in the Panjab.
SUVARNAREKHÁ ...	1. The river Suvarna-riksha, 2. the Kapisá, 3. the Suktimati in Orissa.
SWAT RIVER ...	1. The river Subhavastu, 2. the Suvastu, 3. the Swetá, 4. the Suastos of the Greeks. Pushkalávati stood on this river near its junction with the Kábul river.
SWAT-VALLEY ...	Udyána, south of the Hindu-kush and the Dard country from Chitral to the Indus. It appertained to the ancient country of Gándhára or Gandharva-desa.

T

TAILANGA ...	Same as *Nizam's State.*
TAKHT-I-BHAI ...	Bhimá-sthána of the Mahábhárat and Padma Purán, about thirty miles north-west of Ohind in the Panjab, containing the Yoni-tirtha and the celebrated temple of Bhimá Devi described by Hiuen Tsiang: the temple was situated on an isolated mountain.
TAKHT-I-SULEIMAN ..	Mount Sankarácharya near Srinagar in Kasmir, where Asoka's son Kunála or Jaloka founded a monastery, now called Jyeshtha Rudra, and where the celebrated reformer Sankarácharya established Siva worship.

MODERN NAMES.		ANCIENT NAMES OR SITUATION.
TÁMBRAPARNI	...	The river Támraparni in Tinnivelly. It was celebrated for the pearl-fishery at its mouth even at the time of the Váyu Purán.
TAMLUK	...	1. Támralipta, 2. Támralipti, 3. Dámalipta, 4. Stambapura in the province of Bengal. It was the capital of the ancient Sumha.
TAPTI	...	1. The river Tápi, 2. the Tapani.
TATTA	...	In Sindh. It has been identified by Tod with Dewala ; Cunningham identifies it with Minnagar.
TELINGANA	...	The country between the Godávari and the Krishna : 1. Andhra, 2. Tri-Kalinga.
TENASSERIM	...	1. Tanusri, 2. Tanasseri, the southern division of the province of Lower Burmah.
TEOR	...	1. Traipura of the Mahábhárat, 2. Tripuri, on the river Nerbuda.
THÁNESWAR	...	1. Stháneswara, 2. Sthánutirtha, 3. Samantapanchaka, 4. Kurukshetra, 5. part of the Brahmarshidesa, which comprised Kurukshetra, Matsya, Panchála and Surasena. The ancient Kurukshetra included Tháneswar, Panipat, Sonepat and Amin.
THATUN	...	Sudharmanagara in Pegu on the Sitang river north of Martaban. According to Fergusson it was the Suvarnabhumi of the Mahawanso, and the Golden Cher-

MODERN NAMES.		ANCIENT NAMES OR SITUATION.
		sonese of the classical geographers. Beal, however, identifies Suvarnabhumi with Burmah.
THIBET	...	Himavanta (Asoka's Edicts).
TILPAT	...	Tilaprastha, six miles to the south-east of Toghlakabad and ten miles to the south-east of the Kutab Minar, included in pargana Faridabad.
TINNIVELLY	...	The districts of Tinnivelly and Madura formed the ancient Pándya or Pándu. Its capital was Uragapuram (Negapatam).
TIPPERA	...	1. Katripura, 2 Tripurá, 3. Kiráta-desa, 4 Sundha-desa. The temple of Tripureswari at Udayapur in Hill Tippera is one of the 52 Pithas.
TIRHUT	...	1. Tirabhukti, 2. Videha, 3. Mithilá, 4. Trihuta, the kingdom of Rájá Janaka of the Rámáyana.
TIRUMALA	...	1. Trimalla, 2. Báláji, six miles west of Tripati or Tirupati in the district of North Arcot.
TIRUPATI	...	Tripadi in the province of Madras.
TITTÁ	...	1. The river Trisrotá, 2. the Tritiyá in the district of Rungpur. It rises in the Kanchanjanga mountain.
TONSE	...	I. The river Tamasá in Oudh between the Saraju and the Goomti: it flows through Azamgarh and falls into the Ganges The bank of this river is

MODERN NAMES.	ANCIENT NAMES OR SITUATION.
	associated with the early life of Válmiki, the author of the Rámáyana. II. The river Tamasá in Bundelkhand.
TRAVANCORE	It formed a part of the ancient Chera or Chela. Travancore, part of Malabar and Coimbatoor formed the ancient country of Chera. Travancore was also called Mallára.
TRIMBAK ...	A celebrated place of pilgrimage, called Tryamvaka, near the source of the Godávari, where the sacred tank called Kusávartta is situated. It contains the temple of the Mahádeo Tryamvakeswara, one of the twelve great Lingas of Mahádeva.
TRIPATI ...	Same as *Tirupati*.
TRIVENDRUM ...	Ananta-Padmanábha in Travancore, called from a shrine of Padmanábha. It was visited by Chaitanya.
TRIVENI ...	I. 1. Muktaveni, 2. Dakshina-Prayága, north of Hugli, where the three rivers Gangá, Jamuná and Saraswati separate and flow in different directions after having flowed unitedly from Allahabad, which is therefore called Yuktaveni. II. The junction of the three rivers Jamuna, Chambal and Sindh, between Etawah and Kalpi. III. The junction of the three Cosis, Tamor, Arun and Scon near Náthpur in Purnea.

MODERN NAMES.	ANCIENT NAMES OR SITUATION.
TUNGABHADRA.	1. The river Tungabhadrá, 2. the Tungaveni, a branch of the Krishna, on which Kishkindhyá is situated.

U.

UDAYA-GIRI ...	I. 1. Varáha-giri, 2. Gijjhakuto of the Buddhists, one of the five hills of Rajgir. II. A spur of the Chatushpitha range in Orissa, five miles from Bhuvaneswara. See *Assia range*.
UDAYAPUR ..	I. In Hill Tippera: it is one of the 52 Pithas. II. The Panchápsará lake of the Rámáyana is supposed to have been situated in the district of Udayapur, a tributary state in the Chhota-Nagpur division.
UNDES ...	1. Hunadesa, 2. Hátaka where the lake Mánas-sarovara is situated.

V.

VAIGA ..	The river Kritamálá on which Madurá (Dakshina Mathurá) is situated: it rises in the Malaya mountain.
VÁNA RÁJÁ'S GAR	1. Sonitapura of the Harivansa, 2. Devikota in Gurwal on the bank of the Kedár-Gangá, about six miles from Ushámat and at a short distance from Gupta-Kási, whence Aniruddha, the grandson of Krishna, abducted Ushá, daughter of Rajá Vána.

MODERN NAMES.	ANCIENT NAMES OR SITUATION.
VENGI	Vengipattana, the capital of Andhra, situated on the north-west of Elur lake, between the Godávari and the Krishna.
VIJAYANAGARA ...	I. 1. Hámpi, 2. Vidyánagara on the river Tungabhadra, thirty-six miles north-west of Bellari in the Madras presidency. Sayanácharya or Mádhava, the celebrated commentator of the Vedas, was the minister of Buka Rai, king of Vijayanagara (Thornton and R. C. Dutt). II. 1. Padmávati, 2. Padmapura, 3. Vidyánagara, the birth-place of Bhavabhuti, at the confluence of the Sindh and Párá in Malwa : it was included in the ancient kingdom of Vidarbha.
VINDHYÁCHAL ...	I. The western part of the Vindhya range from the source of the Nerbuda to the Gulf of Kambay, including the Aravali range, was the Páripátra or Páriyátra of the Puráns ; the eastern portion from the Bay of Bengal to the source of the Nerbuda, including the hills of Gondwana, was the Riksha Parvata ; and the range which joins the Páripátra and the Riksha Parvata, including the portion near Bindhyáchal in the district of Mirzapur, was called Suktimána. II. Bindhyáchala, seven miles to the south-west of Mirzapur, celebrated for the temple of the goddess Bindubásini, appertained to the ancient city of Pampápura.

MODERN NAMES.		ANCIENT NAMES OR SITUATION.
VIPULA-GIRI	...	1. Chaityaka-giri, 2. Wepullo of the Buddhists, one of the five hills of Rájgir in the district of Patna.
VISHNUMÁLI	...	The river Kesavati in Nepal.
VISHNU-PRAYÁGA		At the confluence of the Alakánandá and the Dauli (Dudh-Gangá). It is one of the five (Pancha) Prayágas.
VYPAR	...	The river Utpalávati in Tinnivelly.

W

WAIN-GANGA	...	The river Venwá which rises in the Vindhyapáda range and falls into the Godavari.
WARDHA	...	The river Bhadrá, a tributary of the Godavari.
WARRANGAL	...	1. Arunakundapura, 2. Arunakundapattana, the ancient capital of Telingana in Central India.
WESTERN GHÁTS		The northern portion of the Western Gháts was called Sahyádri, the southern portion beyond the Káveri was called Malaya Parvata.

Y

YARKAND RIVER		The river Sitá, on which the town of Yarkand is situated (Beal).

Z

ZAMANIA		Jamadagni-ásrama, the hermitage of Rishi Jamadagni, in the district of

MODERN NAMES.		ANCIENT NAMES OR SITUATION.
		Ghazipur, N.-W. Provinces. The hermitage of the Rishi is also said to have been situated at Khaira-dih, thirty-six miles north-west of Balia (Führer), and also near Máhishmati (modern Maheswar or Mahes) on the bank of the Nerbuda (*Mahábhárat*).
ZARAFSHAN	...	Same as *Yarkand river*.
ZUKUR	...	Same as *Shecroh*: Jushkapura in Kásmir.

www.ingramcontent.com/pod-product-compliance
Lightning Source LLC
Chambersburg PA
CBHW030823270326
41928CB00007B/868

* 9 7 8 3 3 3 7 8 5 9 7 2 5 *